# Rental Property Investing: Build Wealth & Passive Income With Properties, Flipping Houses, Air BnB & How To Manage Your Rentals + 10 Negotiation Tips (Real Estate For Beginners)

By
Unlimited Potential Publications

# Table of Contents

# Introduction

What you are reading right now might be the roadmap to a more prosperous future. And if you're reading this, congratulations on taking the first step and getting your copy of this eBook. You bought this because you have an interest in real estate and think you might have what it takes to become an investor.

Let's get one thing out of the way first and foremost: it's not as easy as you think. In fact, this isn't something that's going to make you thousands, hundreds of thousands, or even millions of dollars tomorrow. It's going to take plenty of work to achieve success.

Still with us? Good. By doing so, you've pre-emptively accepted the fact that it won't be easy.

But you know you have the patience and the willingness to work hard to ensure that you will find success in real estate investing. That's why you've continued on. Because most of the people who picked this book up might have already stopped reading after the second paragraph.

One thing you'll want to realize is when building your real estate empire, it won't take just you to pull it off. It takes the right kind of people at your side to help you out in any way they can. They are experts in their own right.

They are bankers, legal experts, accountants, real estate professionals, and everyone in between. They are right in your downtown area or just a state away. No matter where they are, you may find someone who will help you achieve levels of success in real estate.

## Do you want to make more money than possible?

Let's talk about you for a moment. You're someone who is probably sick of the boring, mundane lifestyle. You get up, work your 9-to-5, come home, eat dinner, relax, and sleep. Then you repeat the process over again for five days a week.

Sure, the paycheck may bring steady and slightly predictable income. Yet, it may not seem like enough to pay the bills or go on vacation. You feel like trading your time for money is just the nature of life.

But guess what? We live in an age where people are making their own money and working their own hours. They are doing it in so many ways.

People will scoff and say, ‘well that’s not a real job’. Let’s face it, doing business isn’t something for everyone. And not everyone is cut out for it.

However, don’t let someone else’s limited beliefs discourage you. You can make as much money as you like without slaving away at a 9-to-5. But you still do need to put in the work for it.

What better way to jumpstart your income like investing in rental properties? Yes, becoming a landlord may just be the one thing you can do to generate the income that you want so you can be able to do what you want with it.

## Why real estate?

You’re probably thinking about making money. You want to start some kind of business so you can make your own income and become your own boss. It’s possible to do just that.

And it can be done with real estate. The reason why real estate is so popular in terms of making money is simple. People are looking for a place to live or operate their business.

And most people would rather rent a place to live as opposed to purchasing it. Eventually, your tenants may become homeowners themselves. But for now, they have the financial means to rent a place from you.

Rental properties are pretty much everywhere. It's a matter of finding one that will yield a good return on your investment. You will learn how to find the right property later on in this book.

## Who are we?

This is a book based on the knowledge and information gathered by those who have invested in rental properties and have made a good amount of money doing it. They know the ins and outs. They know what to do in order to acquire properties.

Other than that, they will share with you the strategies and tactics you can do to find a piece of property that is perfect for renting out. We'll also show you ways to secure financing as well. And we'll show you how to build your real estate network from the ground up.

## The Benefits of Rental Properties

While building your rental property empire, you'll be putting in quite a bit of work. However, the rewards at the end are pretty sweet. What exactly are the benefits?

Here's what you'll enjoy:

- **More passive income:** You'll be earning more money. If you work hard and follow the proper steps, you may even acquire enough properties to make even more money as you go. Imagine making the same amount of money you make a year, but you make it in a month's time.

- **You'll understand deeply about real estate:** Whether you know little to nothing about it, you'll have a basic understanding of it by the time you have finished reading this book. Plus, you'll be able to gain more knowledge from it when you reach out to other real estate professionals.

- **You'll know the process about tenancy:** You'll learn how tenants apply for a rental space, move in, sign the lease agreements, and move out. Of course, let's not forget all the in-between things that go along with it.

- **You'll learn the ins and outs of business:** Having rental properties will be like a business. You'll understand how to operate it as such using ways to acquire properties, marketing your vacancies, fulfilling the demand for rental properties, calculating your cash flow, and more. Believe us, it's more exciting than you think.

## Where to go from here?

At this point, you know of the benefits. You won't be able to enjoy them unless you follow everything you learn in this book. This isn't something that you read about and use the material to converse with your friends.

Almost everything you'll read about in this book has actionable steps that you can take to assure yourself great success in real estate. It won't work unless you put it into action. It's as simple as that.

From here, you now have two choices: one, do you just decide that rental properties aren't going to be right for you? Or two, be willing to put in the work, be proactive, and make the necessary moves to ensure you acquire your first property and make money?

Remember, this is an opportunity for you to say goodbye to the mediocre 9-to-5 lifestyle and say hello to financial freedom. At the end of the day, the choice is yours. If you are ready to accept the challenge, let's turn the page to begin Chapter 1.

# Chapter 1: First Time Doing A Real Estate Business? Then Start Learning Now

Starting a real estate business isn't easy. It requires time, work, commitment, and dedication. If you're reading this after the introduction, you may have known that and have accepted the challenge.

With that said, stick with us. Because we'll be showing you the ins and outs about starting a real estate business. You'll learn about what you need to know and the kind of people you want to connect yourself with as you start out.

Let's get one thing out of the way: running a real estate business as a one-person band is almost next to impossible. You'll need a good amount of people helping you out along the way. That's why it's important to build a good solid network (which we will elaborate on more later on in the chapter).

And as always, it's good to look before you leap. Especially when starting a new business. We'll explain why later.

In the meantime, let's get started:

## Starting A Real Estate Business and What You Should Know About It

Before diving into the idea of starting a real estate business, you need to know what it's all about. You have to know what you are getting into and what the whole thing entails. Everyone that gets into the real estate business has a certain set of goals that they want to achieve.

Perhaps they are looking for an extra stream of income. Or maybe they are looking to get into a new industry after spending time doing business in another. Each person is different, and their goals are unique.

There is a certainty that you will make money if you run the business properly. How you go about using that money will be up to you. You can set aside money for yourself and set another amount for re-investing in other properties.

One thing to know is that of those who have declared over a million dollars or more on their taxes, about 71 percent of them had been involved in the real estate business in some way. So, there may be some sweet tax benefits that you can take advantage of along the way.

With that said, let's cover a few basic things that you need to know about starting a real estate business:

## Is a real estate business profitable?

The short answer: yes. However, there is a caveat. You can make it profitable so long as you are able to be smart with your assets.

Let's explain this in a brief example: let's say that you want to make money in real estate by increasing the value of the property.

### Flipping or Rehabbing

One good way to do it is to find a house that might need a little TLC (or a fixer-upper if you will). This is known as 'flipping' or 'rehabbing'. And it's one of the fastest ways to make bank when it comes to real estate.

In fact, you can actually do this repeatedly using a method known as BRRRR. If you don't know what that means, no worries. The next chapter will have a section explaining it in further detail. At this point, the property value has no place to go but up.

But there's another caveat: you have to put in the money to improve the property's overall quality. This means that there needs to be repairs and maintenance that need to be done to the property you have purchased.

This means setting off money to the side that will go towards any initial repairs (including unexpected ones when something else is discovered). Granted, you don't have to do all the repair work and the like yourself. You can hire professional contractors to get the job done for you.

After all is said and done, the fixer upper is looking better than ever. From there, you can rent the place out to tenants or have it appraised prior to selling it outright. So, the value of the property will be way better than before you acquired it.

## Profits Through Income

Another way to make your real estate business a lot more profitable is by acquiring properties and renting them out to tenants. These properties can either be residential or commercial. Since you are most likely new to the game, you should be better off acquiring residential properties.

However, you could acquire a commercial property assuming you have the cash. Just remember, while the rent for commercial properties will be even higher, the expenses will be higher as well (compared to residential properties). But to make it easier, go with residential properties for now.

You can collect rent by renting out apartment units or even single-family homes (among other property types). Keep in mind that aside from the income portion, you'll also need to factor in expenses as well. These include insurance, property management fees, any loan payments, and so on.

## What are some other things you need to know?

Now that you have a good understanding on how to acquire profits, it's time to discuss what is also known as the other 'moving parts'. These are some things that you'll want to keep in mind while you are starting a real estate business.

It's important to implement some of these steps and not skip through them. Not only because it will allow you maximum results. But missing pieces of the business puzzle will make things a bit more disorganized.

Plus, running the business will be frustrating enough. So, let's lay out some things before moving further:

### Know your business goals

When it comes to success, it takes planning. Succeeding in business by way of some 'shot in the dark' strategy will be impossible from the get-go. So, you'll want to plan and prioritize what needs to be done when it comes to your business goals.

What are your personal goals? What about your professional and financial goals? How do they all tie together?

These goals should influence you to start and build a real estate business from the ground up. Also, consider looking ahead. Where do you plan to be in five, ten, or even twenty years?

How will you get to where you want to be in those time frames? That's when you need to strategize, evaluate, and even make some changes if needed. The goals you set will keep you focused while allowing you to take action on them.

One kind of goal framework to adopt is the SMART framework. This stands for Specific, Measurable, Attainable, Relevant, and Time-Bound. You want to use this framework for both short-term and long-term goals.

### Do your research

This is a big one here. Research is important especially when you are starting a real estate business. Particularly when you want to scope out the first ever property you want to acquire.

Your research has to be in-depth and detailed. When doing this research, you have to gather some pertinent information. This includes the median home values, rental prices, amenities in the neighborhood, and more. Simply put, it all comes down to your financial goals and the kind of real estate you want to acquire.

So, if you are looking for single-home fixer uppers, find an area where you might be able to find one. Or if you are looking into commercial real estate, then your local downtown area will always be a good place to start. Either way, doing research and putting in the time to find the right kind of property will be important.

In fact, we would go so far to say that you should NEVER skip this step. Because a lack of research and preparation will lead to one bad deal after another. You want a positive return on investment, not a negative one.

## Keep your finances in order

Your finances must be in good shape. Especially when there's a good chance you may need to borrow money from banks or lenders. This means making sure that your credit score is in good standing.

Yes, there are ways to acquire financing. And you can get involved in real estate without putting down a single penny. However, it's better to be prepared for all possible options than never.

You want to take a look at your existing accounts and current investments. If you have any debts that need to be paid off, focus on doing so before even making the first major move in your real estate business. Being able to straighten out your financial affairs might put you in a better position to get approved (or even pre-approved) for a loan.

## Sharpen your business strategy

After getting your finances in order and doing plenty of research, it's time to lay out the business strategy itself. This includes writing out a business plan that includes all the tools and resources you plan on leveraging from the start.

Your business plan should include your mission statement, marketing strategy, and what the initial income and expenses will be among others.

## Form a Real Estate LLC

An LLC is a business structure that is set up so your business costs don't interfere with your personal finances. This is a great way to keep your finances separate so your real estate properties don't involve any personal reliability. Depending on your state, there will be different fees and regulations that will be tied into establishing an LLC.

However, the concept will usually be the same. This includes the following:

- Confirming the state's regulations
- Choosing a unique business name
- Filing an Article of Organization with your state
- Creation of an operating agreement
- Publishing an intent to file (if required)
- Application of a tax ID number via the IRS.

## Plan your marketing strategy

You can market your real estate business using various channels. But it's important to know what your unique value proposition is. What makes you stand out amongst the other competitors in your industry?

Also, you may want to consider the idea of putting together a mission statement and the core values of your business (which should be included in your business plan). You'll want to come in with a battle plan on how you want to reach out to your potential customers.

Here are some marketing approaches to consider when marketing:

- **Direct mail:** This marketing method is tried and true. And it still reigns supreme in the Digital Age. Direct mail has become more of a 'road less traveled' method because many people are using digital marketing.

- **Email campaigns:** If you have an email list of potential leads, this method would be perfect. You can send emails to potential buyers or sellers of property that you are interested in acquiring. List building is important, and it will take time to put one together. But other than that, it's one of the best (if not most cost-effective) ways to market your business.

- **Social media:** Because it's the Digital Age, every business owner and their mother will be using social media to market something. So, it will become hyper competitive at best. However, you can spread out your marketing on various social media channels like

Facebook, Instagram, Twitter, or even LinkedIn. It all depends on who your initial buyers are and where they frequent on social media.

- **Networking:** If there is one reliable marketing channel that will assure you success in real estate, it's networking. Where do you begin? See if there is a real estate event in your area. If there is one, attend it. Meet real estate professionals that know their stuff. They will also be more than happy to help you get started with your own real estate business.

## Five Benefits for Starting A Real Estate Business

What are the five benefits for starting your own real estate business? Here's what they are:

- **Tax benefits galore:** Those who are in real estate will take advantage of so many tax benefits when it comes time to file. You get to keep more of your money compared to someone who has grossed the same amount of money working a regular job. Crazy, right? The government tends to reward real estate investors better than those who work a 9 to 5 (which makes quitting it a lot more appealing once you get money rolling in).

- **Cash flow:** Of course, you can get a good amount of cash flow coming in. The cash flow is the money you get once all of your income and expenses have been factored in. This is extra money that you can keep to yourself or reinvest it in other properties. It's your call either way. The more properties you own, the greater your cash flow.

- **Appreciation of value:** The property you own can also appreciate in value. This can happen by paying off any loan you may have that's tied to the property. Despite the fact that the economy can go in one direction or the other (including the housing market), the property value will appreciate over time regardless.

- **Control of the property:** You own it, you control it. There's no better way to say it. The property is tied to you, not some other Company CEO, Wall Street banker, and so on. So, do what you want with it (so long as it's within the legal parameters).

- **Security in retirement/finances:** If there is one thing that you might be aiming for, it is financial security. Your real estate portfolio might be part of your entire retirement plan.

The more financially secure you are for the future, the better. And what better opportunity to acquire more security by putting together a real estate business?

## There Are Many Ways to Invest Your Money in Real Estate

As mentioned before, there are two major ways to invest money in real estate. You can make money with the 'flip' or 'rehab' approach. The other way is by rental income.

But did you know that there are other ways to invest your money in real estate? Let's take a look at some of the other ways to go about putting your money in real estate and seeing a good return on investment:

- **Mortgage notes:** This is a great way to ensure that you have some passive income. You can buy a mortgage note and receive monthly payments that also include the interest and the principle. In a sense, it's like receiving income as if you are renting out a property. The good thing about mortgage notes is that you can invest in real estate without having to jump through so many hoops like real estate licensing, taxes, or abiding by local regulations and the like.

- **Real Estate Investment Trusts (or REITs):** Like mortgage notes, REITs allow you to invest in real estate without even buying or managing a property. REITs are publicly traded and can also be available in non-tradable forms. However, the SEC highly discourages non-traded REITs because of the high fees, illiquidity, and the potential that they could become worthless over time. Publicly traded REITs are liquid and can provide you with a dividend.

- **Real Estate ETFs and Mutual Funds:** You can purchase exchange-traded funds or ETFs and mutual funds that may be based on specific sectors. One of those sectors of course is in real estate. There are mutual funds that specialize in real estate development or even property management firms. Like REITs, these are highly liquid, and the costs are usually low.

- **Using the 1031 Exchange:** The 1031 Exchange involves like-kind properties. The number 1031 is based on the tax code allowing you to sell a real estate property and using the funds to purchase another property with value that is equal or greater. Sometimes, you may take advantage of the exchange and find a property that is more profitable than your previous one.

- **Refinancing:** You can refinance your mortgage if you so choose to do so. One awesome benefit you can get out of it is you can easily obtain a loan with lower interest. Another benefit? Lower mortgage payments.

## The People You'll Meet Once You Get Started

You will be getting in touch with people that will help you through the process of building your real estate business. We will go over who you'll meet and why they're important in Chapter 4. These are people who are knowledgeable in more ways than one when it comes to investing and maintaining your real estate properties.

## Get Your Head Straight Before You Jump In

Yes, there is real money involved. And yes, you can stand to get a substantial amount to the point where you are financially secure for the rest of your life. However, you need to do one thing before you jump into the real estate business.

Here are some tips that you absolutely need to take to heart before getting into it all:

## Keep your emotions in check

There is nothing more thrilling than getting money in the bank (even if it's five or six figures a month) from real estate. However, you can get caught up in what may be an 'expected outcome' and fail miserably to the point where you might give it up. However, it's important to get into the business with a level head.

So, it's better for you to know the numbers and determine if it's the right investment or not rather than just say 'yes' without thinking twice. It's better to use your gut rather than your emotions.

## Accept the fact that you need to put in the time

Building a real estate business from the ground up takes time. And by this, we don't mean putting in an hour here or an hour there. And it also doesn't mean going into research mode constantly (meaning you read all this info and never apply it). As far as time is concerned, this will be a long-term thing.

How long exactly? About a year or even 18 months tops. So, you need to accept the fact that you've got to be in it for the long haul in order to succeed.

## Never stop trying and don't give up

Failure only happens when you give up. Yes, there will be setbacks. There will be shortcomings.

But it's all part of the process. Just because one property seller or a loan lender says 'no', it's not the end of the world. There's an opportunity waiting to be taken every day of the week. And there are those so oblivious to it that they don't know it's staring at them in the face.

So, take that opportunity when you see it. But make sure you do your due diligence, so you know it's the right one to take.

## Focus on one thing at a time

It's true that you can overload yourself. Whether it's focusing on too many tasks or real estate opportunities, it's better to stand back, take a deep breath and focus on one thing. Many of us were not made to be juggling so many things at once.

When you focus on one thing at a time, your focus will be invested heavily on that one thing. You can pay attention to other things at some point. But focus on the priority tasks and the like first before all else.

## Final Thoughts

If this is your first foray into real estate, the sooner you start learning the ins and outs, the better. Starting a real estate business is no easy task. And it won't just take one person to get the job done.

There are many ways to make money through real estate. But your most common ways of doing so is by flipping properties or renting them out and earning monthly income. Putting together a business plan with a solid list of goals and keeping your finances in order is key.

Also, the benefits will be even more awesome once you're in the thick of it. Just remember, you need to keep your emotions in check and accept the fact that building a real estate business from scratch will take time, effort, and yes even money.

But don't let the tasks intimidate you. This will separate you from those who want to try something just to make a quick buck, but give up after finding out how complicated things are. You're in it for the long haul and you want to attain success no matter what.

If you are in it to win it, then there's no turning back now. At this point, you can accept the challenge and move on to the next chapter. Or you can just say ‘you know what, this ain’t for me’ and move on to something else.

In the event it is the latter, stop reading this now. Otherwise, accept the challenge, keep reading, and let’s talk about choosing a rental property and why getting cold feet is the last thing you ever want to deal with. Let’s move forward and get moving.

# Chapter 2: You're Choosing Rental Property Investing? Don't Get Cold Feet!

Now that you have decided to move forward in building your real estate business, there might be little room for turning back now. So, if you are dealing with 'cold feet', you can either press on and find out that it's not so bad to build a business that gives you absolute freedom.

Or, you can focus on something different. Other than that, let's move forward. Because we have a lot to talk about on the subject of rental property investing.

Investing in rental properties is by far one of the best ways to generate profit from a real estate business. All you need are properties like a single-family home, a multi-family home, or even an apartment complex to rent out to tenants. Granted, like any other business that you approach, the task itself isn't easy.

But if you are an absolute beginner, we highly recommend rental properties. Not only will it be easier for you in terms of managing the finances, but you'll also be able to crunch a few numbers while looking at properties to acquire. This 'number crunching' will help you determine whether or not the property will be a good return on your investment.

But we'll talk about the numbers later on. This chapter will focus on rental properties and why it will likely work to your advantage. You'll want to make sure that you are up for the challenge.

Speaking of challenges, we'll talk about those and the difficulties that come with investing in rental properties. They will be brief since we'll touch more on them as we go farther in the book. But once you get a good idea of what you're dealing with, you'll be more than prepared.

Lastly, you know that there is a lot of money to be made. We'll touch on that briefly as well. Finally, we'll talk about how investing in rental properties works (including the moving parts that go along with it).

Let's dive right in and get started:

## Getting Real Deep with Rental Property Investing

As a beginner, there's a good chance (about 80 percent or more) that you'll wind up looking at rental properties. In fact, they will more than likely be the starting point for many real estate property investors like yourself. The reason is simple: you are getting recurring monthly income through tenants via rent payments.

However, you have to understand that with the rewards come the risks. We'll be taking a look at some tips that will help you find your first ever rental property. These tips were made to not be ignored, so pay close attention.

Here's what they are:

## Are you cut out to be a landlord?

This is a simple 'yes' or 'no' question. But before answering it either way, think deep about it for a moment. Are you someone who is a 'handy' person?

Are you up for fixing broken pipes at three in the morning? Or are you willing to hire a property management company to get the job done knowing that it can cost more?

If you answered 'yes' to either of these questions, then there's a good chance that you are cut out to be a landlord. It's up to you whether or not you want to deal with the repairs yourself or outsource them to a contractor or property management company (so long as you have the cash set off to the side). You may be cut out for being a landlord if you have the capability of putting together a team of reliable people who can handle such things with your property like repairs, appraisals, and so on.

## Be sure to pay down any personal debt

Do some investors carry debt? Yes. But that doesn't mean you have to.

We're talking about personal debts here. Student loans, medical bills, or even your kid's college education (assuming you are older and have kids in school). The sooner you pay it off, the better.

## Lock in a down payment

If you are looking to secure a rental property, then it's important to find one where you have enough to lock in a down payment. Keep in mind that some properties will have a larger down payment requirement compared to properties that are considered owner-occupied. How much of a down payment do you need?

Try 20%. The reason why is because there won't be mortgage insurance on rental properties. For example, if the rental property is roughly $200,000 to buy out right then you'll need at least $40,000 for the down payment.

You can secure this money usually through a bank loan. You can easily be pre-approved so long as you have no serious debts (we weren't joking about personal debts and why you need to pay them off).

## Location, location, location

This is the one word you'll keep hearing until the day you're done with real estate (or when you die). Either way, the big 'L' word that pertains to rental properties is location. You want to pay attention to what might be the best location possible in terms of a good return on investment.

Your property should be in an area where it's on the up and up rather than declining. When you are looking for a rental property, there are some factors that need to come into play. For example, what are the amenities in the neighborhood?

Furthermore, how low are the property taxes? What's the average commute time for most residents? The deeper you dig, the more data you'll gather on the area and whether or not it would be a good place to find a rental property.

The location of the rental property will have an effect on the overall value itself. There is no need for you to choose a property located on a rough end of town because it's cheap and you want to save money.

Remember, all the amenities and positives you can find because of the location will often mean a larger pool of potential tenants.

## Buy or finance: what is better?

If you have enough cash to purchase a property outright, then it's obvious that 'buy' is the clear choice. If you don't have enough cash to purchase a property outright, then financing would be your next best option. However, in terms of the latter, you'll want to take a look at your options.

Also, it will depend on your business goals. For example, if you are looking to make money by the flip/rehab way, then you'll want to consider a hard money loan for financing purposes. We'll explain the best way to go about doing this in a later chapter.

For everything else, there's always the personal loans. You put down 20% for the down payment, and then you have other expenses like the mortgage, operating expenses, and so on. Consider your ROI when figuring out which option is better for you.

If you choose the financing route, this next tip may apply to you:

## Stay clear of high interest rates

Did you know that interest rates for rental properties are higher than traditional mortgages? Now that you do, it's important to find a mortgage that has lower monthly payments. That way, it won't have to eat a lot into your monthly profits.

## Crunch the numbers (like ROI margins)

The goal for a positive ROI should be around 10 percent. Keep this in mind when you are crunching numbers while searching for the right property. Another thing to keep in mind is the maintenance costs, which should be at least one percent annually of the property's value.

When calculating to find the right margin, also take into account the other expenses like property taxes, HOA fees (if applicable), insurance, property management, repairs, and so on.

## Don't forget to factor in unexpected costs

Things happen at any time, day, or night. For this reason, it's good to plug in the figures that will be enough to cover any kind of unexpected costs. How much should you set off to the side each month? Consider at least 20 to 30 percent of your rental income.

## Prepare Yourself: Are You Up for The Challenge?

Whether it's one rental property or five of them, there will be challenges. And each property might have its own challenges. One may need urgent repairs while another is dealing with a pest problem.

So, it goes to show you that not all properties will always have the same challenges. But there are challenges that can start before, during, or after you have tenants occupying the property. We will be diving deep into these challenges later on in the book.

But the most common ones will be covered right now. They include:

- **Repairs and maintenance:** These might be needed at any time whether a tenant occupies the property or not. The cause for these never takes a day off, nor does it care if the property is occupied or not. Be prepared for any needed repairs, small or large.

- **Unreliable tenants:** There are two kinds of tenants: those who pay on time and those who don't. This is where a screening process for tenants is handy. You can do this by yourself or via a property management firm.

- **Financial challenges:** These will exist no matter how far along of the journey you're on. You might get rejected for a loan, have tenants skipping out on rent, or sinking in a lot of money into repairs. They come in different shapes and sizes. So you best be aware of them.

## Why Rental Property Investing Is for You?

There are plenty of reasons why rental properties are perfect for beginners like you. And we'll take a look at the reasons why shortly. Rental properties do have their advantages and disadvantages. But they are a lot easier to manage and maintain.

Aside from that, here are a few other reasons:

### You're in control

Simply put, you own the property, and you can do what you please. It's not tied down by anyone else, nor will you be restrained from making such decisions by banks or other entities. This means you're in control of how much you can charge for rent (within reason), how to use the property, and so on.

## Appreciation of property

The property that you acquire will appreciate over time. And you can use what is known as leverage. This is explained as using a small amount of money for a down payment or the like, while borrowing the rest in multiples ranging from four to twenty times more of the purchasing price.

An example of how leverage works is this: Let's say you use $20,000 of your own money and borrow $80,000. This means you can buy property that is $100,000. Your property may appreciate by a percentage over the next 10 or so years. The appreciation will be on the entire asset, not your own money.

## More money for you

Isn't it nice to have a little extra money in your pocket? Well, the good news is that it is possible when you have rental properties of your own. But remember, it all comes down to the income and expenses.

Take the monthly income with the expenses and there is your cash flow. If you are in the positive, that's good. If you're in the negative, you may want to consider making adjustments to the expenses that you are spending on. While we're on the subject of expenses, set aside 5 percent a piece on monthly maintenance and vacancy costs.

## Tax write-offs

Rental property owners will get plenty of tax deductions. What qualifies as tax write-offs? Let's take a look at the following:

- Interest paid on the mortgage
- Insurance policy
- Travel expenses (if you own properties outside of where you reside)
- Property taxes
- Maintenance repairs

It goes to show you that it pays to have rental property. Whether it's just the one or multiple, things will tip the scale in your favor if you are smart with your finances and rely on those who can handle things like the day-to-day property management and other things that one person obviously cannot do.

## You're Going to Make A Lot of Money with This Business

It's possible that you will make a lot of money with a real estate business. Especially if your portfolio consists of just rental properties. However, don't expect to get rich overnight with just one rental property.

But there are plenty of benefits that you will get out of this. The positive cash flow, the tax benefits, and so on. Obviously, this will go without the usual downsides like unreliable tenants, unexpected repairs, and the like.

We'll be talking about the whole money-making aspect of running a real estate business later in the book. But consider this section a brief synopsis of one of the biggest benefits that you can get out of it. Plus, we don't want to divulge any further details or spoil it for you.

## An Overview of How Rental Property Investing Works

To give you a good idea of how the entire process works, this list will be an overview of how rental properties work. Pay attention to this as this can serve as one of your roadmaps to success. We'll also use a similar approach when the time comes to talk about the BRRRR approach.

In the meantime, here's how the process typically works:

## 1. Purchase the property

You find the property that you are interested in after doing some analysis. This includes the kind of ROI you'll get in total after factoring in the income and expenses. You'll also need to find out if the property is in a good location and is valuable enough to be a good investment.

## 2. Do any necessary repairs or renovations

Nine times out of ten, you're going to need to do a thorough inspection of the property itself. If you find anything that needs to be fixed, take care of it as soon as possible. Furthermore, you'll need to determine if there is a need for any renovations.

From there, get as much done as you can in terms of these repairs or renovations. You can do them yourself or hire a contractor to do it for you.

### 3. Rent out the property

Afterwards, you can rent out the property to tenants. It's important to market your vacancies wherever there is high traffic. You can advertise by social media or use old school approaches like direct mail or flyers.

When you are accepting applications, field through them to determine who would make a great tenant. We highly recommend background checks and doing reference checks as well. It would be a lot easier if you hired a property management firm to do this for you.

### 4. Hold on to it and collect income

You might have long-term plans as far as holding on to the property is concerned. You can generate income so long as you own the property yourself. You also have the option to refinance the property so you can easily obtain another loan and acquire subsequent properties.

Once again, we'll discuss that later on when we discuss the BRRRR strategy.

## 5. Keep the financials in check

Throughout the month, you want to regularly check the financials to see that you are still maintaining a positive cash flow. Vacancies can be filled or unfilled from month to month or depending on the length of the lease. If the income and expenses are the same, keep moving forward.

But it's better to double check your finances to see if there is anything amiss. You'll never know what will happen between one day and the next.

# Final Thoughts

Rental properties are a no brainer, even for the newbie real estate investor. Yes, there are some pros and cons to it. But you'll be able to handle them properly with patience, due diligence, and the ability to delegate any responsibilities if needed.

Rental properties are a great way to jumpstart your bank account once you're in the real estate business. And your entire portfolio will probably consist mostly of them. You can have apartment buildings, single-family homes, and even a few commercial properties.

It is important to do your due diligence first and foremost to ensure that the property you're interested in is worth it. One piece of property may yield a negative ROI because of the conditions of the surrounding area. Or the property may be in disrepair.

Your property value may even get dragged down even if it looks better than the surrounding buildings. That's why choosing a location is important. And you also want to take a look at what's close by in terms of amenities, the commute time, and so on.

Don't let the tasks and responsibilities of owning a rental property intimidate you. So long as you play it smart and stick with it for the long haul, success will be assured.

# Chapter 3: Make Sure That Your Finances Are Straight, This Is No Get Rich Quick Scheme

Repeat the following: 'I will get my finances in order before moving any further.' Again. One more time.

We cannot stress this enough. Before you even make the first major step in starting your real estate investment business, you have to make sure your finances are in strong shape. That means taking a look at your personal debts and paying them down to a point where they can be manageable (or paid off altogether).

Also, a reminder that your real estate business is no 'get rich quick scheme'. Don't expect a million dollars to magically appear in your bank account the day after you acquire your first rental property. In the words of that famous commercial, 'that's not how any of this works'.

Even after your finances are in good enough shape, you still have to deal with the financing aspects of the real estate business. Applying for loans, dealing with rejections, and so on. After that, there's still the

balancing act of finding the right cash flow after factoring in the income and expenses.
This chapter will answer all your burning questions about the financials when you're starting out. Questions like, 'How much is this going to cost me?' or 'do I need a reserve fund?'...and similar questions like that.

By the time you finish up this chapter, you will have at least a basic understanding of the financial aspect of the real estate business (specifically things you'll need to know about loans and the like). We'll also be talking more about the numbers and how to crunch them together so you can get a good deal out of every agreement you jump into.

Let's sharpen those pencils, dust off those calculators (you'll need them later), and get right to it:

## How Much Will It Cost You?

This is the million-dollar question that every aspiring real estate investor asks. Granted, the answer probably isn't a million dollars. Before we move any further, let's make a quick adjustment of the mindset.

If you are planning to make money in real estate, don't consider spending money on things as something that's going to 'cost' you. Think of it as an investment for something better. So instead of asking 'how much will it cost me', ask yourself 'how much will I invest'.

Get the idea? You're investing in your future long before investing in your first property. As for the question of how much you'll need to invest, the answer is 'it depends'.

It will depend on the expenses that you are willing to spend. Some of them are completely optional. And there are those expenses that are so necessary that you'd be crazy to not spend money on them. What are some of the costs that are considered necessary?

Let's take a look at the following costs that you should consider with rental properties:

- **Down Payment of loan and interest:** Unless you intend to purchase the property outright, the next best thing would be to consider a down payment on the loan plus interest. As mentioned earlier, the down payment will usually be 20 percent of the purchase price. On top of that, you'll also want to put down an extra percent for the interest itself. If you really want to play it safe, consider 25 percent as the down payment.

- **Property taxes:** Of course, property taxes are a necessary evil. And it will vary depending on the property that you purchase. It will also depend on where you live. And one more thing, this is one expense that could increase or decrease without warning. If you want to stay ahead of the curve, you may want to pay attention to what your local and state governments are doing (even if you hate politics).

- **Maintenance:** This is one of those required expenses that you'd be insane to forego. Indeed, things happen anytime, no matter what they are. One good rule of thumb is to set aside a total of 10 to 12 months' worth of rent to cover these costs. If you want to talk percentages, budget anywhere between 10 to 15 percent of the annual rent. For example, if you have 20 units renting out at $1000 per month ($20,000), you'll earn $240,000 annually in rent. Therefore, the annual reserves should have $24,000 to $36,000.

- **Insurance:** The insurance policy you get will depend on factors like where you live and the kind of property it can cover. When considering insurance policies, consider some of the environmental problems that occur on a regular basis. If you live close to major bodies of water, get a policy that covers floods. If you live in an area that's prone to wildfires, you better get a policy that covers fire damage. Also, discuss rates with insurance representatives and find the best policy that works in your favor.

- **Association (HOA) Fees:** If your property has an HOA formed, then there will be additional fees. As such, make sure that they are included in your budget. If you want to avoid them, find a property that is not under the jurisdiction of an HOA.

- **Utilities:** This is somewhat optional. You can defer the utility payments to the tenant, or you can include it within the rental agreement of what it will cover. If you intend to cover utilities in your rental agreement, you'll need to get estimates from the utility companies to get an idea of how much gas, electricity, water, etc. is used per month.

- **Looking for tenants:** Yes, finding tenants to fulfill your vacancies will eventually be an investment. For this reason, it would be a good idea to provide a non-refundable application fee to offset any costs. $25 would be a good place to start and some even command higher application fees. This is typical of property management companies that own several apartment buildings.

- **Vacancies:** In the world of real estate, you'll always be dealing with people coming in and people going out. So, vacancies will be common. However, there is no telling how long a vacancy will stay vacant. You might want to set aside one to two percent of the property value every year. Do not assume that your vacancies will be fulfilled every month of the year. You can allow two months of vacancies at most.

## OK, so what's a good number to keep in mind?

Now that we've covered the costs that you need to consider, what is a specific number that you need to know? How much of a minimum amount do you need to get started? The answer is 20 percent of the property value.

So, if the property value is $100,000, then it will need to be $20,000 upfront. Oh, and keep in mind that there are closing costs that will be around five percent of the purchase price. But remember, you'll need additional money for cash reserves just in case things happen BEFORE you even get around to renting out the property.

## Will You Be Needing A Reserve Fund?

As hinted in the last part of the previous section, the answer is yes. A reserve fund is something you'll build up using money that you set off to the side. This will be useful in the event of unexpected instances such as sudden repairs, unannounced vacancies, and so on.

A reserve fund will also be your saving grace if there are big problems that have suddenly appeared. We're talking things that go beyond the costs of your monthly rental income. If you have a reserve fund that will cover enough of the costs, then you'll want to be in good shape.

It's good to know that you will be prepared for the worst no matter how many properties you own. It should be large enough to cover any of the common, but unexpected issues that happen with rental properties and other real estate. Better to be prepared than never at all.

How much money you'll need to set aside in the reserves will depend on several factors. These include but are not limited to:

- The property's location
- Age of the property
- Property type
- Number of united
- The last time the property was updated
- Your level of risk aversion

## More specific numbers

Do you want the specific numbers? Well, you'll get them. Because we have a few specific numbers that we want to throw out.

Here are some of our recommendations:

- **$5000 per property:** This is a good starting point for most rental properties. You can grow the number until it reaches $10k to $15k max. To start, you want to use a base and add on a portion of the rental income to ensure more growth. If you want another specific number, you may want to set aside 10 percent of your rental income per month for reserves.

- **If you are less risk averse:** Consider starting off with 3 months' rent in total for your reserves. This should cover at least the required expenses like the mortgage, taxes, interest on the loan, and insurance.

- **If you are more risk averse:** Starting off with 6 months' worth of rent will be enough for those who are risk averse. It will cover the expenses we've mentioned in the previous example and also any additional expenses.

Now that you know some more of the specific numbers, you'll want to refer back to this section if you ever get stuck or run into a financial snag. Sometimes, you might just start off with the less risk averse option just to be on the safe side rather than have more of it as originally intended.

Knowing the best practices of building a reserve fund will help you out immensely in the long run. Because you will run into problems that will require you to use the reserve fund. Over time, you will probably have plenty of it to keep you covered for years.

Imagine having a colossal disaster on your hands and not stressing out about it. Why? Because you know you have the money to take care of it.

If you are going forward without a cash reserve, it's the equivalent to riding a motorbike at night without any headlights. Oh, and it's completely dark too without the moonlight or anything else. In other words, don't go any further without building up a cash reserve.

## How Much Do You Know About Real Estate Financing?

You might know the basics of real estate financing. Or you may not know any of it. Either way, this book will help you understand the terminology that you need to know and understand so you don't get confused or 'fly blind' as you go about starting your real estate business.

In this and the next sections, we'll be going deep into real estate financing, so you'll know things like loan-to-value, loan-to-cost, and so on. But what's so important about financing?

The importance of financing is that it covers the conventional and non-conventional ways of acquiring a rental property. Financing is your best option if purchasing the property outright cannot be done due to being low in funds. Yes, there are ways to finance a rental property including loans.

Keep in mind that there are loans that you can put to good use such as conventional bank loans, hard money loans, and so on. There is also bank and creative financing as well. What's the difference between the two?

Let's take a look at them:

- **Bank financing:** In plain English, you're basically getting a loan from a bank. This is one of the common ways to go about your financing for properties. You apply for a loan, it gets looked over, and you're either approved or rejected. Loan requirements will differ from bank to bank, so that's why you'll need to explore your options rather than be dead set on one financial institution in particular.

- **Creative financing:** The words 'creative financing' is the non-conventional way for financing. This includes approaches like a master lease agreement, seller financing, and personal loans to name a few. These financing options will vary in terms of the credit requirements, flexibility of the loan term, and even the processing speed.

The important thing to remember is that you'll want to invest in a property that will give you a positive cash flow. Otherwise, you'll be in a much deeper financial hole. And it may be hard to pay back the loans if you have a property that is generating a negative return on investment.

## Get A Good Understanding of Loan-To-Value and Loan-To-Cost

What is the difference between a loan-to-value and a loan-to-cost? We'll delve into that further in this section. We'll weigh the pros and cons of each, so you'll know what to expect.

Also being discussed is the loan-to-after repair value or ARV. In the meantime, let's dive right in and discuss it all:

## Loan-to-Value explained

The loan-to-value ratio or LTV is what is used when you're determining the amount that is necessary for a down payment. This will also determine whether or not a lender will extend a line of credit to a borrower. If the LTV ratio is at or below 80 percent, borrowers can apply for the lowest interest rates possible when financing for a property.

In order to understand the LTV ratio, this means understanding the formula that makes it up. Here's what you need to do:

- To get the LTV ratio, you have to divide the mortgage amount over the appraised property value. Therefore, the formula looks like this: **LTV = MA/APV**

For example, let's say the property that you want to acquire has an appraisal value of $200,000. The down payment is $40,000. So now, you'll need to borrow $160,000.

**160,000/200,000 = .8 (80%)**

Therefore, 160,000/200,000 comes out to .8 or 80 percent. So, you're right at the ideal LTV ratio. Again, if the ratio is at 80 or below, you'll be in good shape in terms of paying off the loan with low interest rates.

Let's try another example. Let's say the rental property is the same price, but the down payment is double ($80,000). Since you put down $80k, then all you need is $120,000 to borrow.

Now, let's crunch the numbers:

**120,000/200,000 = .6 (or 60%)**

As you probably notice, the higher the down payment, the lower the ratio will be. However, if you are a low-income borrower, obviously the LTV will be higher. There are lenders that have mortgage programs for these types of borrowers including Fannie Mae and Freddie Mac (among others).

## How the LTV is used

The LTV will be used by lenders to offer mortgage and home equity borrowers the lowest interest rates possible. If the LTV is higher than 80 percent, it will not exclude any borrowers from being approved. The only difference is that they may pay more in interest compared to someone who has a lower LTV.

If your LTV ends up being above 80 percent, you should strongly consider private mortgage insurance. Keep in mind that this may add up to anywhere between 0.5 to 1 percent annually on the total loan amount. These PMI payments will be required until you manage to reduce the LTV to 80 percent or less.

Also, the LTV ratio will work in your favor in terms of your loan application. The lower it is, the better. But that isn't a guarantee.

## Pros of an LTV

- The lower, the better in terms of interest rates and easy loan approval
- Reduces over time with PMI payments
- A high LTV will not mean rejection of a loan application

## Cons of an LTV

- It does not include any additional mortgages like a second mortgage or a home equity loan

## Loan-To-Cost Ratio

Now, we'll discuss the Loan-To-Cost ratio (LTC). Without wasting time, let's break down the formula of the LTC ratio:

**LTC = Loan Amount/Construction Cost**

A higher LTC will mean that the project will be much more of a risk for lenders. Lenders will only finance projects that have an LTC of up to 80 percent (there's that magic number again). Like the LTV, the lower it is from 80, the better.

The LTC will usually come in handy if the rental property is more of a commercial real estate project. So, what does the LTC ratio tell you? This is determined to calculate the percentage of the loan amount that the lender will be willing to provide when you want financing.

Let's take a look at the LTC formula at work:

Suppose you have a commercial real estate project with construction costs ranging out to $250,000. Let's say the lender provides you a loan for $200,000. So:

**200,000/250,000 = 80 percent (or .8)**

In this instance, $200,000 seems like a risk to borrow since the LTC is right at the limit. Therefore, the less money the lender gives you, the lower the LTC will be. However, if the construction costs are higher, that's when the LTC gets reduced.

## What's the difference between the Loan-to-Cost and the Loan-to-Value ratio?

Both the LTC and LTV ratios are similar to one another. But there are slight differences. The LTV is a comparison of the total loan given for a project that goes against the value of the finished project (after repairs and renovations).

The LTC is based on the future value of the project once it is completed. One common way to determine the value is by doubling the hard costs. In our example above, the hard costs were $250,000.

Let's say the total loan was $350,000. So:

**350000/500000 = .7 (or 70 percent)**

So, the LTV ratio of the project is 70 percent. Not bad at all.

### The Pros of the LTC Ratio

- The size of the loan will be based on the total cost of the project as opposed to the appraised value. Actual costs will give the lenders more accurate data

- LTC provides the borrower with funding based on the expectation of what they're spending on construction costs and the like

### The Cons of the LTC Ratio

- The cost for construction and renovation for each project is usually difficult to determine at the outset

- Loan amounts based on the LTC could be smaller than loans that use an ARV. This can be due to the property's estimated value once repairs have been completed.

## Loan-after-repair value (or ARV) explained

The ARV or the after-repair value is defined as the value of the property after it has been repaired or rehabbed. Obviously, the value will differ when compared to the condition before repairs. Here's the formula that you want to use to determine the ARV:

**Purchase Price + Value from Renovations = ARV**

One rule that you need to abide by is the '70% rule'. The bid price for property must not exceed 70 percent of the ARV minus the estimated repair costs. The reason why this is the rule of thumb is because it will allow real estate investors to make an ROI of 30 percent.

So the formula is like this:

**(ARVx70) - Estimated Repairs = Maximum Purchase Target**

So, let's plug in some numbers:

Suppose the value of the property after repairs is $500,000. And the cost of repairs will be roughly $75,000. Let's calculate the maximum price:

**$500,000 X 70 percent - $75,000 = $275,000**

Therefore, the maximum purchase target is $275,000. Do not pay any more of the maximum purchase target than you need to, or you'll end up bleeding cash.

## Real Estate Financing Options that You Should Know

There are plenty of financing options that are available for real estate. Earlier, we mentioned two of them: bank financing and creative financing.

There are other financing options that we'll be taking a look at as well.

Without further ado, let's dive right in:

## Creative Financing

Starting with the non-conventional way of financing, we'll dig deeper into creative financing. This is intended for a real estate investor to purchase a property under a certain situation. Specifically, if the investor in question has bad credit or a credit history that can easily disqualify them from a standard loan, creative financing is the best possible route.

If your credit history is shot, then this might be the clear option going forward. What kind of creative financing techniques are available to you? Let's take a look at a list:

- Private loans
- Lease options
- Credit partners
- Loans from IRA owners
- Equity partnerships
- Purchases that are subject to the mortgage

What makes this option even more appealing is that it's flexible, fast, and can work in any market condition. So, if the market is good or bad, creative financing will still work to your advantage. On top of that, there is no limit to how many loans you can have (so long as you pay them off in a timely manner).

As well as that, creative financial methods are not as risky. So, you won't need to put anything up for collateral unlike bank loans. This may seem like the easiest route to take if you want to waste little or no time with bank applications.

If you have straightened out your finances and paid off debts, you can try and give this kind of financing a shot. But when it comes to your own finances, just because it's for those with bad credit and the like, doesn't mean you shouldn't pay off debts.

## Conventional Bank Loans

This is the common road that real estate investors take whenever they are in good financial standing. Meaning their credit is in good shape and they have shown that they are reliable in paying back the loan. As mentioned before, conventional bank loans require a 20 percent down payment of the property you are purchasing.

Your personal credit history and credit score will determine whether or not you get approved for the loan or not. However, financial institutions will differ in terms of the qualifications that you'll need to meet for a loan. The more stable your credit and payment history is, the better your chances are of getting approved.

### Hard money or 'fix-and-flip' loans

Hard money or 'fix-and-flip' loans are short term loans that carry high interest rates. So, you'll need to put it to good use and fast. The best way to do it is by using the money to purchase a property, repair or rehab it, and then sell it or rent it out.

Then, you can refinance the property and pay off the loan in time. We'll dig a lot deeper into this when we talk about the BRRRR method. Hard money loans will be easy to acquire despite the fact that your credit and income get checked anyways.

The interest rate for these loans can go as high as 18 percent and can depend on the lender. If you have a list of hard loan lenders on hand, be sure to consider the interest rate as one of the driving forces behind your final decision.

## How Leverage Works in Real Estate

Leverage is using money that you borrow to purchase property. The way this works is that you purchase the property rather than cover the purchase price outright. And it's one of the reasons why it's one of the best ways to finance your real estate projects.

The intent behind leverage for real estate is you'll want to be able to increase your returns with money that you are borrowing without putting in a lot of your own money into it. It will allow you to purchase a property that costs more than the amount that's available or have it distributed across multiple properties in your portfolio.

You can use leverage if you don't have enough cash to purchase your target property outright. Or you can do it in order to maximize your returns while putting less of your own cash into the property itself.

Either way, leverage can work to your advantage if you are smart with it. However, there are risks that you need to avoid. Let's take a look at what they are:

## High payments = high leverage

The truth is that you want to keep your expenses low. High payments for a loan will equal high leverage. And that will eat into your finances or risk putting you in an even greater financial quandary if things go south.

If you are unable to make the payments, you'll find yourself in a much deeper hole. So be sure to pay your monthly payments on time and make sure they are low and reasonable.

## Depending on high levels of appreciation

Yes, property will appreciate over time. But don't count on it and shoot yourself in the foot. If you do so, you may overpay on properties.

One thing that you need to do is plan out your investments that are leveraged and sort them out by three different scenarios: best, worst, and most likely.

## Allowing good financing to lead to a bad purchase

Plenty of investors have overpaid for properties. Why? Because they think that high-leverage financing was the best thing to do.

However, it's quite the opposite. Even with a little cash outlay, not every property would be considered a good purchase. You'll want to take a look at the property and consider the current and expected market trends, respectively.

You'll want to make sure whether or not the property is overpriced or if there is any room for appreciation. If the room for appreciation is little to none, then you want to consider finding another property. Otherwise, you're in deep trouble.

### Forgetting about cash flow

At the end of the day, it's all about the cash flow. And if you overpay or use leverage improperly, that cash flow won't flow as freely as you think. If your investments take a nosedive, you'll be losing money instead of gaining it.

## Brush Up Your Math, You'll Be Needing It

Sure, math probably wasn't your favorite subject in school. But what you might not realize is that it holds the most value in so many ways. Especially when you'll be doing some real estate investing.

You don't have to be a math genius to crunch some numbers and determine whether or not you're getting in on a good investment or not. Everything you'll use math wise is simple enough as it is. We'll be taking a look at a few math formulas that you'll need to ensure that you can properly crunch the numbers while searching for your first and subsequent properties.

We'll make these as simple as possible because we're not huge fans of complicated math formulas. But rest assured, these formulas you need to know about won't stress you out in the slightest.

Let's begin with the first one:

## 1. Price to Rent Ratio

The price to rent ratio will be the average property price divided by the average rental income. Therefore, the formula looks like this:

**Average Property Price/Average Annual Rental Income = Price to Rent Ratio**

The goal here is to find a property that is financially sound in terms of investing in it. You'll want to find a low price to rent ratio (typically anywhere between 1 to 15). If the ratio is anywhere north of 15, then you may want to consider affordable properties that will help keep it low.

## 2. The Net Operating Income (NOI)

This is basically another name for the word 'cash flow'. The net operating income is the amount of income that you get using the following formula:

**Monthly gross income - monthly expenses = NOI**

Chances are the income will be from rent paid by your tenants. And you also might have additional income from the property itself including pet fees, income from laundry, vending machines, or any other amenities that charge a fee. There are different kinds of non-rent income that you can consider to ensure that your NOI is in the positive.

## 3. Cash-on-Cash return (COC)

The Cash-on-Cash return or COC is roughly the same as the ROI calculation (which we will get to in a bit). The COC is calculated as follows:

**Annual pre-tax cash flow / total cash invested = COC**

The number you get from this is an indication of what you might expect on your investment. However, it should not always be a reliable figure as it may differ from the actual ROI itself. The reason being is because you are using cash flow figures that do not include taxes.

It also does not include mortgage amortization. This COC model should be used if you are focusing on a yearly ROI.

## 4. Capitalization Rate (Cap Rate)

The Cap Rate is the ratio between the net operating income and the sale price. Therefore, the formula is this:

**NOI/Sale Price = Cap Rate**

For example, let's say your net operating income is $20,000 a month. But we'll be gunning for a cap rate using the annual monthly income. Divide that by the sale price (let's say $500,000) and you get the cap rate.

So, for example, this is what you do:

**$20,000 x 12 = $240,000**

**$240,000 / $500,000 = .48 (or 48%)**

So the cap rate is 48 percent. With this cap rate, you'll expect at least a 48 percent return on investment. Not too shabby. However, if the cap rate goes up, then the price/earnings valuation multiple will decrease.

The cap rate is a great tool to determine whether or not the property you want to invest in will yield a good ROI.

## 5. Cash flow

The cash flow is definitely something you want to include in your figures for obvious reasons. To calculate the cash flow, you take the net operating income and minus by the debt service (not the expenses). Bet you didn't expect that, did you? But it's true. So here's the formula:

**NOI - Debt Service = Cash flow**

What exactly is the debt service? You are subtracting the NOI with the amount you repay if you have a loan.

## 6. Return on Investment (ROI)

The return on investment is your cash flow divided by the cash you invested in the property. So, let's say the cash flow you have after subtracting the NOI from the debt service is $12,000 per month. But you are shooting for an annual figure. Therefore, $12,000 times 12 is $144,000. Let's calculate the rest with the amount you've invested in the property (we'll say $300,000):

**$144,000/$300,000 = .48 (48 percent)**

So for example, if you already invested $300,000 into the property and take in $144,000 in NOI every year, that's a 48 percent investment. Again, not a bad number to have.

### Note: Use online calculators if needed

To help you save time and perhaps money, you should consider using online calculators to help you get accurate numbers for cash flow, ROI, cap rate, and so on. Check out the following calculators from these sites:

https://www.calculator.net/real-estate-calculator.html

https://www.fortunebuilders.com/real-estate-calculator/

## Final Thoughts

Your finances must be in good shape even before you start considering the type of financing you need for your real estate properties. Even after you've acquired your first property and have tenants moving in, it's important to make sure that your finances are in order.

You absolutely need to consider having a cash reserve handy in the event that you run into any unexpected expenses along the way. The same goes once you have things up and running. It doesn't matter if you own one or five properties, having cash reserves handy is the smart thing to do.

Also, keep the equations listed above in mind. Especially when you are looking for a property that will generate monthly income. Get to know some of the equations like the Loan-To-Value ratio (LTV) or the Loan to Cost (LTC).

Don't forget, you'll also need to consider the loan-after-repair ratio should you be dealing with properties that need a little fixing up after being acquired. Also, leverage is your friend when it comes to investing in properties (only when done right). Lastly, don't forget to factor in things like cash flow, return on investment, the cap rate, and so on. Crunching numbers is all part of the game.

Even if you hate math, it will serve as your useful ally whenever you have the goal of making money in real estate. It will even be your best friend that will help you get out of a potentially bad investment (while saving you money in the process). Take your time with these calculations and be sure to focus on one of them at a time.

Lastly, keep the minimum and maximum numbers in mind (like the LTV and LTC). The lower the maximum number (i.e. -- 80 percent) the better. However, if you are looking at ROI, the higher the number, the better.

# Chapter 4: Hiring and Working with the Important People of Your Real Estate Team

As we have said before, real estate investing is dang near impossible to do as a one-person band. That's where your real estate team comes in handy. In this chapter, we're going to show you how to hire the people that will be perfect for your team.

It's obvious that you need more than a pair of hands, eyes, and ears to help you find the best property to invest in. You may think that it's hard to do. However, you may not have to start too far off to find people who you can trust and are willing to help you grow as a real estate investor.

We'll talk about how to find people such as a property manager, an attorney that can handle all your legal affairs, who to go through for insurance and so on. These are people who will likely stick with you in the long term. The key here is to choose your people wisely.

In business, you may think that you've hired the right people. However, when tensions mount and tempers flare, then it gets to the point where you have two people not speaking to each other for an indefinite amount of time. So, who do you hire?

Let's answer that question and then some right now:

## Start Looking Within Your Family

Before you say anything, there is nothing wrong with a family operated business. And let's not talk about stuff like nepotism or the like. That's totally off the topic.

But if you are looking for people that will help your business grow, you don't have to look any further than your own family. However, considering such an option requires you to look over a few things. For example, is it legal to hire family members?

The answer: it depends. But you'll want to check out any federal, state, or even local laws that will allow or prohibit family members being hired by you as an employer. This is one of the many reasons why you'll want an attorney as part of your team overall.

They will be knowledgeable of the laws in question. They will point out which laws allow family members to work together (or the laws saying otherwise). Another legal thing to look at is child labor laws.

You cannot simply have minors under a certain age working for your company. That's when you need to review the federal, state, and local laws pertaining to this. If you have a child that is of the minimum labor law age, then you may consider a small role for them (like groundskeeping).

Also, take a look at the IRS tax policies regarding family members as your employees. For example, you can withhold income tax if you employ a parent or spouse. However, you cannot withhold FUTA taxes from their income itself (with the exception if your child is 21 years old or older).

## The Pros and Cons of Hiring Family

When hiring family members, you'll want to know about the pros and cons in general. What will be the positives of having family on your real estate team? What will be the liabilities?

Let's take a look at them right now:

### Pros:

- **They have strengths and weaknesses:** You might have a family member that can capitalize on a few strengths that they may have. And they also might have some weaknesses that you know about. You can help them capitalize on the former by assigning them a role that they know they'll be competent at. Do you have a member of the family that can work the books with ease? Hire them as a bookkeeper. Do they have a good eye for property acquisition? Hire them as one of your scots.

- **You know who to include on the team:** You are well aware of the skill sets that your family members have. There are members of your family that will have a skill or two that will benefit your business. However, there are others in your family that possess irrelevant skills that will not help your business out at all.

## Cons:

- **Some family members do not have the skills:** The truth is, you have family members that won't be a good fit for your business. And that's what you need to understand right off the bat. That's because they won't know what they're doing or will even be qualified for such a job.

- **Your other employees may not appreciate it:** The word 'nepotism' might get flown around a lot. Some employees may resent you for the fact that you have family on staff. And thus, they blame their lack of opportunities solely on that. Regardless, treat all employees the same way whether they are family or not.

- **Unproductive family members:** Lack of productivity really brings down a business. And for that reason, they'll fall behind on various tasks. As such, you may have a family member that may be hired for something but doesn't put in the amount of work that they're supposed to. At this point, it's either have them work as much as the rest of the employees or cut them loose.

The truth is you can start with family as your employees. However, you'll want to make sure you are hiring the right family members. Pay close attention to what they're strengths are and determine whether or not they will be beneficial for your business.

## Accountability Partner is Not Only for Fitness Purposes

If you are looking for someone who will help you propel your real estate business, it's an accountability partner. This is someone who will help you keep yourself accountable whenever you need to meet a certain set of goals (be it short-term or long-term). Accountability partners are not just for fitness purposes anymore.

You can have an accountability partner who will help you in the long haul get from zero to six figures over time. Do not confuse them for mentors. These are people who know you can get from point A to point B, but want to make sure that you get there.

## What to Look for in an Accountability Partner?

So, what exactly do you need to look for in a reliable accountability partner? Let's take a look at a few characteristics that will make one stand out over the others that may have potential:

**Genuinity:** Having a genuine friend as your accountability partner is a plus. Why is that? Because they can respect you not just as an individual, but also as a business person. They know of your hopes, dreams, and aspirations. And they will do their best to help you get there.

**Availability:** You and your accountability partner must realize that you both have to be respectful of each other's time. You don't want someone who will be busy all the time. And you definitely don't want anyone that will never make time for you. If you need someone to talk to, make sure that you have an accountability partner that will always have time to chat with you if you run into any problems or concerns.

**Clarity, honesty, and tact:** You want someone who is not afraid to be honest with you. At the same time, you want someone who will give you a straight answer rather than beat around the bush. This is what separates some of the best accountability partners from those who may be considered 'wishy-washy'. Straight, clear, and to the point is what you'll want from an accountability partner.

**Similar industry, different perspective:** Keep this mantra in mind when looking for an accountability partner. They need to be in a similar industry, so they have a clue about what they are doing. At the same time, you want them to be looking at your goals and aspirations from another angle. This way, they can help you incorporate various strategies including where to invest and whether or not the area itself is viable for a good ROI.

## Why should you have an accountability partner?

Having an accountability partner is a must whenever you want to build a business. There are three reasons why you would want one on your side each and every time. Let's take a look at them:

- **Your partner will keep you on track:** The one true thing that an accountability partner does is keep you on track. That's it. They help you stay on track with your goals and complete the tasks that need to be done day after day.

- **They are willing to be a gauge for success:** Your accountability partner wants you to succeed. They also want to let you know how close you are getting to succeeding. You can also measure each other's success and compare.

- **They help you become smarter:** They will help you become more knowledgeable in real estate. They will relay 'need to know' information. And they will keep you in the know of things when it comes to real estate news and so on. But they want you to be aware of it so you can make any necessary changes, if needed.

## Agents, Brokers, and Realtors

We'll be talking about agents, brokers, and realtors and the roles they play. We'll also talk about the differences in responsibilities and how they earn money. Take a closer look at each one:

**Agents:** Real estate agents are people who are licensed to assist in buying, selling, or renting properties. One of their chief responsibilities is bringing the buyer and seller together to ensure that a deal is done. In addition, their responsibilities include carrying offers and counteroffers and making sure that both clients are aware of any requirements that need to be met before the deal is approved. Real estate agents get paid by commission fees. While they may not get the entire commission, it's usually split up as follows: Listing agent, buyer's agent, the listing agent's broker, and the buyer's agent's broker. For example, if the commission is 8 percent, all four parties will get 2 percent a piece.

**Brokers:** Real estate brokers do pretty much the same tasks as real estate investors. Brokers will work with buyers in terms of looking for property based on the criteria set by their own clients. There are also seller brokers that are responsible for determining market values of the property that their client wants to sell.

At the same time, they use listings and show properties to buyers including those that are being sold by their client. There are three types of brokers: associate brokers, managing brokers, and principal or designated brokers.

Brokers typically get paid by taking a share of the commissions earned by the real estate agents that work for them. Brokers can make their own deals and therefore do not need to split their own commissions.

**Realtors:** Realtors are professionals in the industry and are members of the National Association of Realtors or NAR. One of the main things that gets confusing is that realtors and real estate agents are considered the same. However, there are some differences. To become a realtor, they must have a real estate license that is valid and active. And they must be active in the business itself. They must also have no sanctions based on unprofessional conduct and also have no pending or recent bankruptcies. Realtors get paid based on commission and will usually have it split between other agents.

## Finding A Real Estate Professional

Now, it's time to find a real estate professional that you can trust. The question is: who will you want to be a part of your team? Do you want a real estate agent or a broker? Or do you want a realtor who may have a deep network of real estate professionals that you can leverage if and when needed?

The first question is where to find them. Let's take a look at some of our recommended methods in finding a good real estate professional:

- **Ask your friends or family**

- **Do online research (i.e.: [Your City] + Real Estate Agents)**

- **Attend open houses in your local area**
- **Drive around the neighborhood (and see who's selling houses along with the realtor they are going through)**

## Characteristics to look for while finding a real estate professional

When you are looking for a real estate professional, the ultimate goal is to find someone you can trust. This means that you'll have to find one that has these characteristics that we'll list below. With that said, here's what you need to look for:

- **Someone who is a problem solver:** When it comes to creating solutions, a real estate professional does just that. They know how to make a property more marketable for buyers or investors.

- **They are self-motivated:** Like you, they are self-motivated entrepreneurs that are hungry for success. It takes drive, determination, and smart decision making for both of you in order to get where you need to be.

- **Honest and have integrity:** Obviously a huge factor here. If they have honesty and integrity, you'll be better off giving them your trust. However, don't dive in just yet. You want to be sure you are working with the right person. And you want to make sure whether or not they are going to screw you out of a good deal.

- **They have an interest in houses and architecture:** Most of those who are in real estate have some sort of interest in houses and architecture. So, they're not just in it for the paycheck. With knowledge about the houses and the kind of architecture and design, they are reflected as more professional and an expert on all things houses in the eyes of the buyer or seller.

- **An engaging personality:** They are someone that is willing to have a conservation with someone. They are patient, always willing to ask or answer questions, and connect with people who are interested in purchasing a property or selling one.

- **Attention to detail:** Real estate agents need to pay close attention to detail. If they are able to, they will have a long and successful real estate career. And they can be one of your most trusted members of your real estate team.

- **They understand the housing market:** Whether it's the broad market or the local market, the real estate professional you want to partner up with is someone who understands it. This will help them give you a good idea on when it's the right time to purchase a piece of property and what part of the local area to steer clear from.

- **A robust network:** There is no doubt that a real estate professional will have a network of people. Not only will it have other real estate professionals, but everyone else from property managers, lenders, attorneys, and so on. They will gladly refer you to people within their network if there is a need that you want fulfilled.

## Working with One

Once you've found a real estate professional, you'll want to know how to work with them. At the same time, you always want to make sure that you are working with the right person. You want someone that you can trust and will never screw you over.

When speaking with a real estate professional that you are interested in working with, it's important that you ask questions. Gauge their knowledge of the real estate business and the housing market. Do they sound like they know what they are talking about or do they sound like an idiot?

Also, are there any pre-existing connections between you and the real estate professional? If they are related to your family in any way, don't choose them. And simply don't choose them because you grew up down the street from them either.

It all comes down to someone who is experienced in the field and also has a professional reputation. So yes, it's better to be picky about which real estate professional you want to work with before you hit the ground running.

## What about 'double agents'?

Double agents are just something you hear about in spy movies. There are such things as dual agents in real estate. In rare cases, they do work.

But nine times out of ten, you want to steer clear from them. Not only are they not good to work with, but in eight states (Alaska, Colorado, Florida, Kansas, Maryland, Oklahoma, Texas, and Vermont), being a dual agent is against the law. Who is a dual agent you ask?

A dual agent is someone who is a real estate agent that represents both the buyer and the seller in a transaction. However, this will create all kinds of problems as it can create some conflicts of interest. If anything, avoiding 'dual agents' will be key when you want to invest in real estate.

Instead, you want to go with an exclusive agent. They need to be exclusive to buyers or sellers. If you want to buy properties, a buyer's agent will obviously be your go-to person. When it comes time to sell the property, a seller's agent should be somewhere in your network.

## When to get rid of a real estate professional?

Hopefully, the real estate professional that you choose is someone that you can trust and will always be honest and transparent with you. However, if they are causing you problems, it's better to let them go rather than keep them around.

However, you want to think this decision through before doing anything else. It's better to repair a relationship first to see if both you and the real estate professional are on the same page. They may have a style or performance that you may not agree with.

Or they may have failed to meet certain expectations. Iron out the wrinkles before doing anything else. If all else fails, that's when you notify the professional that you want to terminate the working contract between the two of you.

To help avoid problems, you want to do your due diligence on the real estate agents that you are interested in working with. Keep a close eye on what they're saying and take notes. It will come down to who you want to work with based on experience, competence, and credibility.

## Hiring A Property Manager versus Self-Management

The next most valuable person on your team is a property manager. This is someone who will help handle tenant issues on your behalf. Plus, they are also responsible for determining which tenants can rent your properties and who cannot based on the policies and conditions that you set forth.

Of course, you have the option of managing the property yourself. This means you handle all the tenant applications and decisions. Plus, you have other responsibilities such as getting in contact with the right people in the event you need repairs or some other issues taken care of.

What option will work best for you in the long run? That would depend on how much work you are willing to handle. Let's take a look at some differences between property management versus self-management:

## Property management

### Pros

- A property manager does the heavy lifting, so you don't have to. It makes your work as a property investor a lot easier. Plus, it's less stressful

- They are well aware of the market and will usually handle the nooks and crannies of property management

- They can handle problem tenants, so you don't have to. Especially when it comes to missed payments, damage to the property, and so on.

- Often useful when you own numerous properties. So long as they manage them well, your properties will be in good shape.

### Cons

- With property management, it comes as an additional expense. It might be a necessary evil if you choose not to manage the property yourself.

- You might end up with a property manager who may be incompetent and not know what they're doing. So, it's best to screen for property managers should you go that route.

- Some property managers may not meet your expectations. They may be subpar in performance and manage the properties in a way that you did not ask for them to do.

## Self-Management

### Pros

- You can save property management fees

- You can manage it better than anyone else, if you believe you can

- You have even greater control over the tenants that occupy your properties

- You'll have top priority over the property (especially if it's the only one you own)

### Cons

- Self-management is no easy task. This includes chasing down late payments, possible late-night calls about urgent repairs, and performing inspections that happen from time to time

- You might not have up-to-date information that may be needed for tax and legal purposes

- Your real estate resources may be limited compared to those who opt to have someone else manage the property

After looking over this list of pros and cons, it's up to you to determine which will be better for you in the long run. If you don't want to juggle a lot of responsibilities, chances are the property management option will be more suited for you. However, if you have just a couple of properties within the same area, you may try your hand at self-management.

If you plan on owning multiple properties over the course of your lifetime, property management will always be the smart decision going forward. You cannot be everywhere all at once. Plus, you may have property that is hundreds of miles away from where you are.

## Being Insured Can Lessen the Burden

Making sure that your rental properties are insured will be one of your priority tasks as a real estate investor. Disaster can strike anytime and anyplace. On top of that, the damage may be greater than you would expect.

What does insurance cover anyways? When looking for an insurance policy, it's important to find something that will cover the following:

- Floods
- Fires
- Natural disasters
- Damages beyond the control of tenants or owners

The more your insurance policy covers, the better. The reason why insurance is worth looking at (and worth purchasing) is because it will soften the blow in terms of any incidental expenses. Without insurance, the repairs and maintenance will take a considerable bite out of your cash flow.

In order to get a property insured, the first thing you want to do is shop around. Which property insurance policy will serve you best in the long run? And if you plan on owning multiple properties, can you cover them under the same policy?

Let's take a look at some additional tips that will help you find the right insurance policy:

## Know the kind of coverage that you're getting

Insurance policies don't just cover things like the disasters that can cause damages. But you'll need to have your bases covered. You'll want things like liability coverage and even loss of rent coverage (especially if the property becomes uninhabitable for a lengthy period of time).

## Know the different types of rental insurance policies

There are three kinds of rental insurance policies: DP-1, DP-2, and DP-3. DP is short for 'dwelling property'.

So, what's the difference between the three? Let's take a closer look:

**DP-1:** If you are looking for the cheapest form of insurance, DP-1 will be what you'll need. You will get basic coverage. This policy will cover named perils of disasters. If the disaster or peril is not mentioned in the policy, the insurance company will not reimburse you for the damages. Reimbursements will be on an actual cash value basis. The insurer will pay you for any damage except for wear and tear (or depreciation).

**DP-2:** This will give you slightly better coverage compared to DP-1. Like DP-1, named perils that fall under the DP-2 policy will be covered as such. Again, unnamed perils and disasters will not be reimbursed. One major difference is that a DP-2 insurance plan can cover burglary damages while DP-1 may not do so. Insurers will reimburse you for damage based on the current market prices and can do so without taking depreciation into account.

**DP-3:** The most expensive coverage. This will give you the broadest coverage of the three. This will protect you against all perils except those that are excluded in the policy. This will be provided on the basis of a replacement cost.

## Explain to your tenants about renter's insurance

Let's talk about rental insurance for a moment. This is separate from your insurance policy. Your policy is not responsible for any damages to the tenant's possessions. That is why it's important to encourage them to get renter's insurance just in case things happen.

This will lessen their burden after the fact since the insurer will reimburse them for any property that is damaged. You hold your tenants in high regard. So be sure that they are covered in ways that you cannot provide for them.

## How About Those Involved in Fixing?

The final piece of the puzzle in building your team are those who are contractors, handymen, and repair specialists. As mentioned before, damage can occur at any time. And you want some go-to people on your contact list.

When looking for someone who will do the repair and maintenance work, you'll want to find someone who is competent, can do most repairs and maintenance, and also has a good response time.

### Do you need a handyman or a contractor?

There will be times when you will need to ask if a handyman is needed on the property or if you need a contractor. The answer to this question is that it depends. If the repair or maintenance project is small, a handyman will be the go-to person.

One thing to keep in mind is that there may be laws that may allow the kind of work a handyman can do. For example, in California, a handyman is only allowed to do work that totals out to about $500 plus labor and parts. If a handyman does $500+ worth of projects, they must hold a license for a specific area that they focus on.

For example, if a handyman specializes in plumbing and bathroom remodeling, they must have a license as a plumbing contractor. However, a handyman will be useful for small projects.

If the repair, maintenance, or renovation project is large, that's when a contractor will come in handy. Especially if it's a contractor that is focused on a certain area such as plumbing, kitchen remodeling, and so on.

## Hiring a handyman or contractor

If you are considering the idea of hiring a handyman or a contractor, you'll want to take a moment to interview any candidates that you're interested in adding to your team. Ask them about their track record, their areas that they specialize in, and references.

Always make sure that you check with references to see if things check out. You will be around this person on your properties and work closely with them. So, find someone you can trust and have a positive record.

After adding your handyman and contractors, be sure to have a written agreement drawn up so it details the project, the cost, and the frequency of payments. Also, you may want to keep on the lookout for handymen or contractors that ask for a full payment upfront prior to the project.

While hiring a handyman or a contractor may be an extra expense, it might be better if you choose not to manage the property yourself.

## Final Thoughts

Having a team at your side will be important. You'll have the right kind of people who will deal with any issues you may have. At the same time, you have people who specialize in one area of real estate.

Obviously, you'll want to work with a real estate professional who is exclusive to one part of the process, not a dual agent. A property manager might also be a valuable asset if you don't want to perform any self-management tasks. Let's not forget that you'll need someone to take care of the insurance policy just in case things happen.

Finally, when things do happen, you want to have a handyman and contractors in your network. That way, when something needs repairing or maintenance, you can give them a call at any time. These are people who you can trust and will stick with you in the long haul.

Be sure to screen for these people thoroughly so you don't run into any issues. When you do, a big plus is always asking for references. That way, you'll know who you're dealing with and you can make the decision to add them to your team or find someone else.

# Chapter 5: Everything You Need to Know in Finding Houses

One of the best things about a real estate investing business is finding a property that will be great for your portfolio. However, finding the right one can be difficult and it will take time.

This chapter will be focused on what you need to know about finding your first property. You will learn how to use due diligence to your advantage. The farther you go into it, the more you'll know about the property and be able to determine if it's a good find based on the numbers.

Furthermore, we'll be discussing the what, how, where, and who aspects of purchasing a house. Also, don't skip this chapter if you want to overcome your fears of diving into one bad deal after another. Speaking of which, we'll show you how to avoid scams.

We'll also talk about foreclosures and how they might be a good addition to your portfolio. Next, we'll discuss what house hacking is and how it might work to your advantage in real estate. Lastly, you'll learn about why now would be a good time to start creating your real estate network from the ground up.

If you're ready to know more about houses and how you can find one as your first property, let's get going:

## What You Should Know About Due Diligence

With any kind of investing, due diligence is what you usually need to do. You want to make sure that you are looking at the assets in question before you take the great leap with money. This includes stocks, bonds, and yes...even real estate.

Due diligence is defined as an investigation or a review to confirm that the investment you're looking to make is legitimate. You want to double check and make sure that the data is accurate before making an investment. At least 99 percent of the time, doing your due diligence will get you out of a potentially bad deal or a scam deal.

With due diligence, you want to go as deep as you can to get the right information. So, what is the information that you need for real estate transactions? Let's explain what you need to find.

## Due Diligence in Real Estate: What You Need to Know

When it comes to due diligence, it all comes down to the metrics and the types of information you need to have on hand. Each bit of information is different depending on what you're investing in. Due diligence metrics in stocks are way different than those in real estate.

Because of this, we're going to show you metrics on what you need to know when you look at one property. You need to know these numbers (and possibly crunch some of them) in order to determine whether or not it will be a good investment on your end. Let's take a look at the stages of due diligence that need to be performed before an offer is ever made:

### The Neighborhood and Area

**Population:** The population of the area of interest will be key. Because a higher populated area could mean more valuable property. If you are in a major city, there may be suburbs that are closer to the downtown area. A lower populated area could also mean cheaper property values as well.

**Job growth:** If you want a good indicator of how good the housing market is for an area, take a look at the job growth. Is the local economy doing well? Or is it faltering due to layoffs and job loss? If the job growth is negative, you might be second-guessing the idea of investing in a property in such an area.

**Percentage of occupied rental properties:** How many households are occupied by renters? If there are more people renting than buying houses outright, then that could serve as a good opportunity to find a single-family home that you can use for rental purposes.

**Vacancy rates:** How many rental properties are vacant during a calendar year? To calculate this, take a look at the number of days the property has been occupied and divide by 365. For example, if a property has been occupied for 120 days [120/365 = .33] then the vacancy rate is 33 percent. This means for a third of the year, the property has been vacant.

**Median rents:** How much are people paying for rent monthly? What's the average? This will give you a good idea of how much you want to set the rental rate for your property.

**Crime rate:** You want your tenants to feel safe in the area that they are living in. If they are in a high-crime area, then odds are you'll be on the losing end of the deal. Make sure that the crime statistics in your area of interest are accurate.

**Neighborhood and school rankings:** Your tenants may have children that want to go to a good school (and maybe close to where they live). How is the neighborhood overall? Are there amenities nearby? Is it commuter friendly? These will factor into the actual rankings for both neighborhood and schools.

## Pro Forma financial statements

**Gross rental income:** What's the current gross rental income? Will it match up with your intended cash flow target? If necessary, will it mean increasing the rent?

**Additional income info:** What other income is there? Are there fees that the tenants pay? Do they charge late fees for missed rent? Are there any application fees? These are what you need to look for.

**Expenses:** What are the expenses that the current property owner is paying? Utilities? Property management? How much are they setting aside for repairs and maintenance every month?

**Property taxes and insurance:** How much are they paying in property taxes every month (or year)? Are they currently covered under an insurance policy? Can that policy be transferred from one holder to another? Or do you need to get your own?

**Cash reserves:** Does the current property owner have cash reserves? If so, how much?

**Future improvements:** What are some future improvements in the works? How long will they take before completion? What's being added to the property?

## Due diligence after an offer is made

If you think the due diligence is finished after an offer is completed, think again. You still need to do more of it when there's an offer on the table. Here are some things that you need to do as part of the post-offer due diligence:

### Physical inspections

You want to see if the property is in good shape. That's when you want to inspect the entire property from top to bottom. This includes checking to see if the HVAC and plumbing system is in working order.

But it doesn't stop there. You'll also want to take a look at the roof and the structural integrity of the property. Also, see if there has been an inspection for any lead-based paint before 1978. Safety is very important for those who will be occupying your properties (including those with young children).

Depending on where you live, you may need to do an inspection for radon gas or defective drywall (especially if the property was built during the previous decade). If the property is near an area where flooding occurs, you'll want to see if there is any verification of a flood zone. If the property is in danger of being flooded, then you want to consider flood insurance.

## Financial Due Diligence

Next, we go back to the financial side of things. This means taking a look at statements that document profits and losses that are for the current year and date back to the last two years. Also, you want to take a look at the tax returns, income, and expenses of the previous owner (information given to the IRS).

Next, you'll want to take a look at the current rent roll. How many tenants are there and how much are they paying in rent. Then you need to take a look at the lease terms for each tenant. Some leases are different because of the different expiration dates.

You'll also want to pay attention to the other terms of the lease such as the deposit amount or any unique agreements made between the tenant and the previous owner. These unique agreements include but are not limited to discounted rent in exchange for something a tenant can do like landscaping.

You'll also want to look for any additional fees that the previous owner has charged tenants. These include pet fees and deposits. You'll need to compare the pro forma information from your pre-offer due diligence and compare it to the numbers that you have on hand now since they will differ from one another.

Don't forget, you'll also need to take a look at any existing contracts made between the former property owner and any other businesses such as contractors, property management companies, and so on. Also, you'll want to be aware of any repairs and capital improvements that were made prior to the acquisition (along with any invoices or proof of payment on file).

### Check for any loan or legal issues

If your property is under an HOA, you'll want to take a look at any covenants and restrictions ensuring that the property can be rented. You may also want to check for any pending litigation between the previous owner and any former tenants. You also want to make sure that the property appraisal matches the purchase price on the contract.

The last thing you want to do is get yourself in a legal battle for something that you didn't do. Sometimes, a former property owner may pass off their problems onto someone else. This is one of the biggest reasons why doing your due diligence is important.

## The What, the How, and the Where of Finding Houses

In this section, we'll be talking about the 'What, How, and Where' of finding houses. We'll be taking a look at what kind of properties are available for an investor, how you can look for them, and where to look.

This entire section will be chock-full of valuable information that is only designed to be applied. Don't read through this and just keep it there for useless information. This will not work unless you take action.

Knowing what kind of property that's available is half the work. But knowing how to look and where is the other part. Now, let's start off with the 'what' portion of looking for a house:

### What kind?

There are different types of houses that you can own and rent out. We'll be taking a look at what kind of houses you can buy and rent out. Each type is different, but they will provide you with a good amount of income from one or multiple tenants.

Let's take a look at the different types of houses that will make a great rental property for your portfolio:

## Single-family homes

Single-family homes are regular individual houses designed for a single family to occupy. They may apply to some different property classes like luxury homes or even vacation homes. Single family homes consist of a number of bathrooms and bedrooms.

For example, a house with two bedrooms and two bathrooms would be a single-family home. Even a luxury home with 12 bedrooms and eight bathrooms would fall under the category of a single-family home as well. For single-family homes, the lot size and square footage will vary from one property to the next.

You get more space and also the ability to expand if needed. Plus, it offers more privacy for tenants compared to other property types.

However, there are some disadvantages. Some single-family homes may be under an HOA, which means there may be certain rules and restrictions. If the home is in an HOA neighborhood, unfortunately they may not be rented out if the HOA agreement explicitly says so.

## Multi-family homes

Multi-family homes can be a property that includes several units. These units can be rented out separately and you can charge the same amount of rent or slightly more (depending on the measurement of the unit). One thing to be aware of is multi-family homes should not be confused for an apartment complex or the like.

However, there are apartment buildings that can be considered multi-family homes. For this reason, you can still rent out to multiple tenants if you so choose. These multi-family homes can be perfect for generating a good amount of monthly income.

Multi-family housing would be great for getting rental income since you'll be renting out multiple units. At the same time, lenders will be favorable towards those who own multi-family homes (especially if you live in one of the units). You can get financing as if it were a primary home so long as you reside on the property itself.

However, if you want to look at appreciation, multi-family properties don't appreciate as fast as single-family homes. The fees for financing these properties will be even higher. And acquiring a loan for the purpose of purchasing a multi-family home may be even more challenging compared to other properties.

## Townhomes

Townhomes are similar to single-family homes. These are also known as row houses because they have a distinguishable characteristic of being two stories high and at least one wall that is connected to a neighboring property. These townhomes are usually modern, so they can be very attractive for both buyers and even potential tenants.

The great thing about these townhomes is that they may be closer to a more populated area. They will be close by to various amenities and may boast some pretty cool views. If you want a house that is underrated in terms of investment opportunity, a townhome just might be right up your alley.

One of the best things about owning a townhome is that some of the expenses that you normally deal with like maintenance and repair will be reduced. Especially if the townhome development is part of an HOA. Yes, you still will need to incorporate repairs and maintenance in your expenses, but they will be much lower than usual.

However, potential tenants may not be too happy with the shared wall. If privacy is one of their 'make or break' demands, then they will not find a townhome as something they want to live in. If a potential tenant cannot handle a lot of noise, then a townhome won't be for them either. Lastly, townhomes may be expensive to buy depending on the area that you live in.

## Distressed Properties

Distressed properties are houses that are considered fixer-uppers. You can purchase the property for a below market price and then put in the needed repairs and maintenance. Once completed, you can sell the house outright for a higher profit or rent it out and refinance it.

Referring to the BRRRR method as we pointed out in chapter two, you can purchase the property, repair or rehab it, rent it out, and then refinance it so you can pay off any loans or the like. The only place for the valuation of the property to go with distressed properties is up.

One of the downsides with distressed properties is that you might run into some issues that may come as a surprise. This means you may be spending a little more than your expected budget. Also, you'll need to get the repairs and maintenance done in a shorter period of time (especially if you need to pay off a hard money loan).

## Foreclosures

Foreclosures are a great property to snag up for a good price. Later on in this chapter, we'll discuss what they are, how important it is to understand them and how you can acquire one. You'll also learn about the advantages and disadvantages of them as well.

## Retail Properties

Are there properties that will allow you to run a retail business on the lower level while having a habitable living space up top? The answer is yes. And what's great about this is that you can own a retail business while racking up additional income for a rental property.

Or if you don't own the retail business, you can get income from both the business owner and the tenant separately (unless the business owner lives on the same property like an upstairs apartment). Either way, retail properties are a good opportunity to generate income.

However, there are some expenses that you need to keep separate. If there are issues with the retail business, you may be paying higher expenses as if you were tending to a commercial property. But if there are issues with the residential side of the property, then the expenses will be charged like it would with an apartment building or a single-family home.

## How to Look for Rental Properties

Now that you are aware of the type of properties that are available, it's time to figure out how to look for them. In today's digital world, it's easy to find them online. However, you might want to mix it up a bit and perhaps use some offline methods as well.

In this section, we'll show you where exactly you can find these properties using the specific methods below:

### Online tools

Even today, more people are relying on the Internet and even mobile apps. There are dozens of rental listing websites that you can start with. These include Craigslist, NextHome, GottaRent, RentSeeker, Apartments.com, and more.

When using online tools, you can take advantage of the filtering features. This way, you can whittle down the properties that you are looking for based on a certain criteria. If you are looking for single-family homes, you can check out realtor websites or MLS listings via brokers like Coldwell Banker, ReMax, and so on.

## Bulletin boards

Online isn't the only place to find properties that you can buy and rent out. You can check out bulletin boards that are in your local area. These can include high traffic areas like banks, supermarkets, shopping malls, and other local businesses where there are community bulletin boards.

If you are planning on purchasing apartment complexes that provide student housing, consider looking at bulletin boards on college or university campuses.

## Classified ads

Just because the Internet is dominating everything, doesn't mean that classified ads have gone the way of the dinosaur. Your local newspapers will be a good place to start. Also, if you have large regional newspapers that have a statewide or regional coverage area, take a look at those too. Sometimes, you may have to go outside of your local area to find the property that fits your criteria.

### Rental guides

Typically, these guides are free. You can find them on street corners or store entrances if they are available.

### Signs

You know those signs that say 'vacancy' or 'no vacancy'? Yep. You'll be hunting around your area of interest for these signs.

You can find these and other signs like 'for rent' in neighborhoods as well. If you are interested in acquiring any houses or apartments, you can call the owner and ask questions. When will there be vacancies? What is the asking price for the property?

Dig into as much information as you can so you can make an offer at some point in the future should the property of interest be suited for you.

## Where to Look?

Location, location, location. One word said three times over. And you'll be hearing that an awful lot when you build your real estate portfolio.

You won't get tired of it because it's one of the mantras you'll remember while looking for one property after another (assuming you want to invest in more of them). The first thing you need to do is choose an area of interest of a potential market.

Nine times out of ten, most real estate investors will start in their local area. That's because they want to be close by to the property should anything happen. However, that's not always the case.

You can acquire properties from a long distance. Whether it's a hundred miles away or even two states over, there is a property that could fit your personal criteria. All you need to do is hire a property manager to take care of the day-to-day operations and you can collect income and have a nice steady cash flow.

As far as where to look, you'll want to take the following into consideration:

## Cost of housing

You'll want to be in an area where the cost of housing is affordable. This will help determine the potential ROI for investors. At the same time, it will also determine whether or not the property will be useful in terms of being a rental property or otherwise.

One thing to pay attention to is the national average. As of this writing, the national average of purchasing a home is over $272,000.

## Demand and opportunity

If you're an investor, you'll want to find a property in an area where the demand for rental units is high. The higher the demand, the better the opportunity. In order to determine the demand, you'll need to take into account some of the following things: population growth, unemployment rate, rental-rate growth, job opportunities, etc. Also, you'll want to take into account another national average.

In this case, take a look at the unemployment rate nationwide. This will change from month to month as the jobs reports and the unemployment figures are released every first Friday. For example, the jobs report for the month of March will be released on the first Friday of April.

As a real estate investor, you want to mark these days on your calendar especially when you are constantly searching for rental properties.

## What type of neighborhood is the property in?

The types of neighborhoods are usually a thing of personal preference. However, you'll want to consider neighborhoods that are occupied by a specific group of people. These can be families, students, or even young professionals.

No strategy is a 'golden strategy' for all. But you'll want to find a neighborhood that dominates the market for that area. For example, if college rentals are dominating the local housing market, then that's a good opportunity to invest in a student housing complex.

Keep in mind that there may also be downsides to this as well. In the example of student housing, there may be parties that rage on late into the night and may lead to damages because of some rowdy, drunk, revelers. And that may mean more money to set off to the side because of repairs.

## Insurance costs

The insurance costs will differ from one area to the next. In other words, not all locations will be insurable equally. Also, you'll want to take a look at areas that are susceptible to certain disasters. For example, you might find that the insurance policies may be higher for areas that are prone to wildfires.

Insurance policies do not come cheap. Especially when the policies are designed to give you extra coverage because you're in an area where disasters can occur regularly (fire, floods, etc.).

## Walkability

One thing to pay attention to is the walkability of a neighborhood. How easy is it to walk from various stores, public transportation stops, parks, and so on? If it's easily accessible, this can be a huge selling point for investors when looking to fulfill tenant space.

However, the farther the tenant may need to walk, the less walkable it might be. Some won't mind walking a mile to the nearest store. But others will. So, consider any place less than a mile from the property to be walking or biking friendly.

## Nearby amenities

What's close by? Is it a recreational center? A golf course?

Is there anything for the kids? Are there any grocery stores nearby? These are the things that you want to pay attention to.

Again, you want to make sure that it's a 'skip and a hop' away as opposed to a long drive. Because it's more convenient for someone to head out, get in, get out, and head back home in the quickest time possible.

### Public transportation options

Are there any public transportation options in the area? If so, how far are they from the property? What types of transport are available?

If they are near public transportation, that's a huge plus. On top of that, it will command a higher price just for the convenience.

## Avoiding Scams

Scams are all over the place. And you can be sure that in the real estate niche, there is bound to be a scam or two out there that may prey on newbie investors like yourself. That's why you'll want to learn about some of the most common real estate scams that have long sucked in many newbies and left them out to dry.

But knowing us, we've managed to track down some of the most common scams, so you know what they are and how to avoid them. These are some of the most common scams related to real estate:

## Escrow Wire Fraud

This happens when you receive a phone call, email, or text from someone claiming to be from an escrow company. They give you instructions on where to wire escrow funds. These fraudsters even try to make it look real by setting up a website, email address, and phone number.

To protect yourself from this kind of fraud, you'll want to refer back to the original documents that were given to you by your lender. Call the phone numbers and see if the escrow wiring instructions you have received were real. Also, do not click on any links (via email or text) or send money online without verification from an authorized person that is associated with your lender.

## Loan flipping

This involves predatory lenders that claim to refinance mortgages. These scammers are known for charging high fees and often target seniors with memory problems. If you have not requested the help of lenders but they are seeking you out, then you may want to avoid them.

To prevent getting caught up in this kind of scam, work with known banks and lenders. Also, question the fees and penalties that are presented if needed.

## Foreclosure relief

This is the kind of scam that targets those who may be falling behind in their mortgages. Because of public records, the scammers can access this and know who is behind and who isn't. From there, they will call the person up and claim to offer foreclosure relief.

Those who want to avoid this scam must speak with a loan service provider while working to modify your current loan. A scammer who discourages you from talking with your lender is a huge sign that you may be dealing with a scammer.

## Rental scams

These rental scams pop up in places like Facebook or Craigslist. The way this is done is that scammers will use photos from a previous listing or from a different property. This is a scam that is known to target younger persons from age 18 to 29.

One way to be wary of this scam is to be suspicious of anyone who asks for upfront cash before you see the property in person. No landlord or property manager would charge anyone a ridiculous amount of money just for a showing.

## 'We Buy Houses'

There is a scam out there where a firm claims to buy houses while giving you money for it. However, while there are some that may exist and use legitimate means, there are scammers that claim to be 'investors'. They give out all kinds of information that you don't need.

Plus, they ask you to pay an application or evaluation fee. Let's not forget, they also ask for your bank account information. Whatever you do, do not give them anything.

On top of that, do not sign any papers or even the deed to your house without the consultation of your attorney or the escrow company.

## Understanding Foreclosures

Foreclosures happen when the bank evicts a resident after they have missed multiple mortgage payments. It starts with the notice of default, followed by the foreclosure filing, the notice of the sale, and the eviction.

You can get a foreclosure property at a lower price. On top of that, you can close the deal a lot faster. And it will also be a good investment property that you can turn into a rental.

However, one of the greatest disadvantages is that you may never see the home or inspect it before purchase. This means that repairs may be needed once everything is all said and done. Lastly, you also may need a ton of cash to buy it.

## How About House Hacking

House hacking is something that can be done if you are planning on acquiring multi-family properties. For this to happen, you want to reside in one of the units and consider it your primary residence. From there, you can have renters of the other units pay the mortgage and other expenses.

As you can see, the concept is pretty much the same as everything else. You use the rental income and take a portion of it to pay any expenses including the mortgage itself. You can also do this using other strategies to pull it off.

You can even rent the property room by room or even rent out an RV on the driveway of the property. If that isn't a crazy way to do real estate, then we don't know what is.

## Start Creating Your Real Estate Network

Later on in this book, we'll be discussing the creation of your real estate network. Already, you may have a bare bones structure already built in. And from there, you can simply build the network from the ground up.

This network should include your fellow real estate investors. Sure, while some of them may be your competition, they also share similar goals as you do. And you can all learn from each other in terms of how to become better landlords and investors.

Creating a real estate network will take time and effort. And it will also take due diligence as well. That's because you want people in your network that you can trust. And these are people who will help connect you with other people whenever you need a problem solved (and you shall return the favor whenever someone needs something from you).

## Final Thoughts

Finding houses doesn't always have to be difficult. But as long as you know what kind of rental property you are looking for, you'll be in good shape. It's important to know how to look for properties, where to find them, and who to buy them from.

Also, be sure to keep your eyes open for any scams that may exist. The last thing you want is to lose your hard-earned money and never see it again because of a scam or a deal gone wrong.

Remember, purchasing foreclosures may be a good way to acquire properties. However, you may need a little extra cash because of the repairs that may be needed in the long-run. If you are considering the idea of acquiring a multi-family property, consider house hacking as a great way to generate more income.

# Chapter 6: Taking Full Control of The Deals

As a real estate investor, you'll be doing quite a bit of wheeling and dealing. Especially when you're going to build a solid portfolio. In this chapter, we'll be talking about the importance of real estate valuation and appraisals.

You'll understand how important they are and how each property is appraised. You'll learn about the different approaches of valuation and appraisal. You'll even learn how to evaluate deals so you can be sure whether or not it will be profitable on your end.

Before any deal is made, you want to make sure that the property is in good shape. That's when we'll talk about property inspections. This is where you'll approach inspections and how they work from a buyer's point of view.

This will show you exactly how to go about setting up a budget, so you know how much you'll need to spend on repairs and renovations. Every good offer should go without a hitch. So, we'll show you how to go through the process of making an offer and what to avoid while doing so.

Negotiation will also play an important role in getting the best deal. In this chapter, you'll learn 10 different negotiation strategies that you can incorporate while you are looking to get the best deal possible. This will include counteroffers and give you an overview of the closing process.

If you are planning on making a deal that will be below the market value, we'll talk about what you need to look for. And lastly, we'll discuss the closing process, so you know what to expect when the paperwork is prepared, signed, and ready for processing.

This is one of the many all-important chapters that you DO NOT want to skip in this book. Especially when you want every deal to be a good one. Let's get started:

## Real Estate Valuation and Appraisal

Property valuation is a process that determines the economic value of a real estate investment. Here, this will determine what is considered a fair market value of the price itself. Likewise, the seller may be willing to sell his or her property to an informed buyer at a price that may seem to be reasonable for both parties.

Both parties will have relevant information. No one will be forced to buy or sell the property. The property value itself and the selling price are not always equal to each other.

At times, a seller can sell the property right off the bat even if the price is below the fair market value. They may be doing this out of desperation or distress. This may not always happen, but it's good to know nonetheless.

An appraisal is done to determine the value of the property itself. There are three methods of going about doing this. Regardless, the appraisal process will include data that will need to be used such as national, regional, city, and neighborhood averages.

Once the data is gathered, the appraisal process uses the following approaches:

**Approach #1: Sales comparison**

This is an approach often used in the appraisal of single-family homes. This is better known as the market data approach. This will estimate the value of the property and compare it to the value of properties that have similar characteristics.

These properties are known as comparables. To provide an accurate comparison, the following must be taken into account:

- The comparing properties must be similar to one another
- Has been sold in an open and competitive market within the last year
- Sold under usual market conditions.

These three comparables will be used in the appraisal process. Other comparables include size, location, and other relevant features. Also, you'll want to take into account the other qualities such as the age and condition, the date of the sale (and any economic changes between the date of the sale and the current day), location, and physical features.

**Approach #2: Cost Approach**

This approach is used to estimate the value of any properties that have been improved over a period of time. With this method, this will use separate estimates such as the building and the land that the property is built on. Also, this approach will take depreciation into consideration.

Other things that will be taken into consideration is the cost of the repairs and renovations if needed. The current costs will also play a role in this approach. Also, the value of the land as if it were vacant must also be taken into account as well.

**Approach #3: Income capitalization**

This is better known as the income approach. This is a method that is based on two things: the rate of return the investor wants and the net income that is produced by the property of interest. These will be used to estimate the overall value of the property itself (such as apartment complexes and the like). The income capitalization approach is simple and straightforward. And it will determine the potential income and expenses that will go along with this property.

As a newbie to real estate investing, you'll find this to be a very easy approach. You'll be able to determine how much income you can generate from rental rates and the expenses that will be taken out to ensure that you have a positive cash flow every month.

## Evaluating Deals

In this section, we're going to show you how to evaluate every deal so you can determine whether or not it will be profitable on your end. This may require some data and even crunching the numbers. Again, we want you to get the best deal possible each and every time.

You do not want to fly blindly into a deal only to realize that it was a bad deal, and it is too late to turn back. We'll be talking about the kind of information you need to gather, as well as the tools you need to use to gather said info. You'll also learn about the property details and what you'll be getting out of the deal itself.

How can you evaluate a deal? We'll show you how to do it step by step, followed by a few rules that you need to follow while doing so. Let's take a look at what you need to do, first and foremost:

## Gather the property details

The property details include the name of the property, the street address (including the city, state, and zip code), and the square footage. You should also include information for the date that the information was prepared followed by the name of the person preparing the details.

## Calculate the purchase details

You'll want to take a look at the market value, the assessed value and then the purchase price percentage of market value. Other information that needs to be included are the purchase price, the equity at purchase, the down payment, and the mortgage amount. Last but not least, you'll want to include pertinent costs including the closing, renovation, and out of pocket costs.

## Rental information

Take into account the number of rental units that are available in the area of interest. Also, take into account the going rate for rent. The figures you want to put together is the rental rate and the renovation costs (both monthly and annually).
This includes two percent rent of the purchase price and renovation costs. Also, take into account the vacancy rate and also the gross operating income. Another thing you need to do is get the average rent per unit.

For example, let's say you have five units: two of them are $650 per month, one is $850 per month, and the last two are $700 per month. Let's add them up:

- 650 * 2 = $1300
- 850 * 1 = $ 850
- 700 * 2 = $1400

In total, that's $3560. Now divide that by five and you get $712 as a rental average. For the annual average, simply multiply by 12 (which gives you $8544). This is a good opportunity to play around with some rental rates to see what is considered reasonable enough not just for your cash flow, but to ensure that you are getting a good ROI out of the deal.

## Estimated Financials

These estimated financials include the estimated operating expenses, net operating income, annual debt service, and the estimated cash flow (including cash flow per unit). If you want to quickly evaluate each deal, use at least 50 percent as the operating expenses for any property. As an option, you can utilize calculated financials and use specific figures rather than estimated numbers.

For example, you can opt for $500 or $502.01. Likewise, you use $550 or $553. Round it to the nearest $5 dollars if need be. To make it easier, stick with the estimated financials since you may not have an idea of an exact number.

## Other analysis

If you want more numbers to analyze, you can also include one-time prices such as the purchase price per unit, renovated price per unit, the gross rent multiplier, and more. This is also a good time to calculate the cap rate as well.

## When should you purchase the property?

This is where the numbers will give you a good indication. There are some requirements that you need to follow. These may include the following:

- The monthly rent or GSI must exceed two percent of the renovated price.

- The cash flow per unit is $100 or more

- The debt coverage ratio is greater than 1.2

If the property meets the criteria, then that should be a green light to purchase the property. However, if some of the figures do not meet the criteria, recalculate until it does. Or you can move on and find another property that will pass the test.

## Analyzing the property's cash flow

As part of your evaluation, you want to analyze the property's overall cash flow. What does this entail? Let's take a closer look:

**Mortgage payment:** Depending on the lender, you'll factor in things like the property tax and the insurance payments. Typically, these can be paid altogether. However, if you don't pay them along with the mortgage then you'll want to account for these items separately.

**Utilities:** This will usually vary. You can cover utilities such as water, cable, and trash while the tenant will be responsible for the lights. If you acquire a multi-unit property, determine what the tenant will pay out of pocket for utilities while choosing which utilities will be covered under their lease agreement.

**Property management fees:** This will be included should you opt for a property manager to take care of the day-to-day operations. The standard figure for such a fee is 10 percent of the total collected rent. If you collect $1500 in total rent, then the property management fee is $150.

**HOA fees:** If the property is under an HOA, then you'll want to include this fee in your expenses. This may apply if you are renting out townhomes or single-family homes depending on the neighborhood the property is on.

**Vacancy:** Setting aside an amount in the event of vacancies will be a slippery slope. For a specific figure, consider setting off a percentage of cash as if you are dealing with five to ten percent of your units being vacant.

**Maintenance:** Things happen. Almost to the point where they need to be repaired or replaced outright. Set aside at least 10 percent every month as a cash reserve for maintenance and repairs. If the property is an older home, you might want to consider setting aside a little more money per month.

**Rental income:** Self-explanatory. The rental income will be the rent per unit. If you have multiple units, the rental rate per unit may vary.

Remember, the cash flow is the net operating income minus the expenses. For example, if the total net operating income is $1500 per month and the expenses are roughly $650, then the cash flow should be $850. And that's just for one property.

## 5 Rules to Keep in Mind While Evaluating A Property

### 1. When you buy, you make money

To explain this, when you buy an investment property, you are aware that the purchase is about the money you'll get from rent. It's about what you'll get for an ROI. It doesn't matter if the kitchen flooring is linoleum or hardwood.

When you buy, you know of the factors that go into whether or not the property is worth purchasing. Keep in mind that if you choose to find a property on an MLS listing, don't expect the return on investment to be massive. That's because the MLS will allow you to pay 10 to 20 percent less than the listed price.

## 2. Use the 55 percent rule for NOI

If you want to calculate the NOI, this is where your number crunching skills will come in handy. The 55 percent rule will be exercised as follows: Take the gross rent for the year and multiply it by 55 percent (or .55).

Let's take a look at the following example: let's say the gross annual rent is $45000 (assuming you have five units at $750 per month for rent). Now multiply that by 55 percent like so:

**$45000 * .55 = $24750.**

Therefore, your annual NOI will be $24750. The remaining 45 percent will go towards other expenses such as insurance, vacancies, maintenance, utilities, repairs, and so on.

## 3. Use the cap rate for property comparisons

Part of the analysis is pitting one property against the other in a battle to see which one would fare better. Keep in mind that at the end of the day, the numbers never lie. In case you have forgotten the formula for the cap rate, it's the net operating income divided by the purchase price.

So for example, we use the $24750 in the previous example and the purchase price is $300,000. Let's calculate it:

**$24,750/$300,000 = 8 percent**

Ideally, you want the cap rate to be anywhere between 6 to 8 percent. Since the cap rate in this example is 8 percent, that's a good property.

However, let's say that you're looking at a building with 10 units. The gross rent per month is $3,000 (or $36,000 a year). The purchasing price is $450,000.

Here's the calculation:

**$36,000/$450,000 = 8 percent**

Once again, we have a property with an eight percent cap rate. If needed, you'll want to whittle it down to the exact decimal. Sometimes, the smallest number might be the best option even by a razor thin margin.

## 4. Consider a significant down payment if you aim for positive cash flow

Let's say for instance you settle with the property that's $450,000 because it's dead on the money for a cap rate. Keep in mind that the down payment will usually be 20 percent of the purchasing price. In this example, the down payment for this property is $90,000.

If the net operating income per month is $3,000, you'll want the financing cost to be less than that amount. So, you'll want to up the ante a bit. Instead of putting down a 20 percent down payment, opt for 30 percent?

Therefore, put down $135,000 instead of the usual 20 percent. This way, you can get a positive cash flow while giving yourself a head start on the mortgage payment (and you pay it off quicker).

## 5. Minimize your transaction costs

Transaction costs are not the best thing to deal with. Especially when you are making real estate deals. For this reason, you'll want to minimize them as much as possible.

It's not common for real estate investors to spend 15 percent in total. That's five percent for purchasing the property and ten percent when you sell it. For a $450,000 property, that's $67,500 of your money spent the whole way.

The costs may even consume any appreciation value of the property. Even if you put down a good amount of money for your property and sell it quickly, the transaction costs will take up at least half of what you get.

## Property Inspection

If you want to inspect a property, then you want to do this from the buyer's point of view. Home inspections are pretty much the requirement before a sale event takes place (in most situations). Even if the property in question is a fixer-upper, an inspection must be done to ensure how much money you are willing to put in on repairs and renovations alone.

Getting right to it, a home inspection will entail a thorough inspection of both the inside and outside of the property. A home inspector will be looking at the following:

- HVAC and plumbing
- Any appliances that are inside the house (i.e. -- Refrigerator, dishwasher, etc.)
- Electrical system
- Structural integrity including the foundation, walls, roof, etc.
- Outside of the property including the fence, lawn, home exterior, etc.

A property inspection will range between $300 to $600 depending on the size of the property and the rates the home inspector charges. The length of time for an inspection will also depend on the size of the property. Smaller sized properties will take one to two hours max while larger homes will take an upwards of six hours.

When choosing a home inspector, it's important to take a look at things like reviews. How many of them are positive and authentic? What are people saying about them?

Also, you may tap into your existing network of real estate professionals and be referred to one or two of them. That might even be the route you go with subsequent properties as well. As long as you have a real estate professional that you can trust, there's a good chance that you'll take them at their word.

Don't be afraid to ask questions as you and the inspector go through the home. That's because you'll want to assess the damage and get a good figure of how much it will be to repair it. Be sure to note any potential costs that the inspector gives you (if any).

## What happens if a home inspection goes bad?

There's always the chance that a bad home inspection can occur. But keep in mind that 'bad' doesn't necessarily mean dire straits. If one does occur on the property, bailing out may not be the smartest decision.

Even a bad home inspection can be important to buyers. That's because it could give them some more options on what to do with the property (including the kind of financing they need to acquire it). In the event of a home inspection, the seller can be responsible for any repairs or pay you the amount needed for them to be done.

Either way, it's a win-win for you because it lessens the amount of money you spend on repairs overall. You get a credit at closing, but you will still need to pay the remainder of the repairs if and when needed.

## Estimating repairs

During the home inspection, you'll want to get a good idea of how much money you'll need in order to get the repairs completed. Once again, it's always a good idea to walk through the inspection when it's being done on site with the inspector.

Have the inspector give you ballpark estimates, so you have a preliminary budget. Keep in mind that the figures may not always be accurate. You could get the repairs done under or over budget.

In the case of going over budget, this may be due to any discoveries you may find after an inspection. Things can happen in the time between the post-inspection and the sale. So, you want to keep your bases covered if needed.

Take into consideration what needs to be repaired and renovated. While the house value will be increased, the costs will be quite hefty depending on the amount of work that needs to be put in.

## Avoid the Mistakes in Making an Offer

When it comes time to make an offer, you want it to go off without a hitch. This means making sure there are as few mistakes as possible. One false move and it can derail the entire transaction.

Before we unveil the top seven mistakes that you need to avoid, let's take a look at the offer making process itself:

### Get a comparative market analysis (or a CMA)

A CMA will always be used during the offer process. This will help determine the true value of the property in question. Of course, this includes the characteristics such as the square footage, number of bedrooms and bathrooms, and other pertinent information.

Also, you'll want to take a look at which properties are currently on the market, which ones are in escrow, and which ones have a closed escrow. You'll want to go back as far as the last six months. These properties must be located within a minimum of a ½ mile to a max of 1 mile radius.

Pay attention to things like the sold price instead of the list price. Also, pay attention to the adjusted average sales price. You can also compare it to other properties and determine whether or not the units and lots are the same size, if the number of bedrooms and bathrooms are the same as the property you're looking at, if they are close to each other, and so on.

## Look at the market trends

What kind of market is the area in? Is it a buyer's market or a seller's market? You'll know just by taking a look at the neighborhood.

If you hear stories about buyers making multiple offers before one gets accepted, that's when you'll know that it's a sellers' market. If you hear of stories about a buyer getting a great deal on a home that's been on the market for a lengthy period of time, then the market is a buyer's market.

Basically, it takes word of mouth and asking around to determine the kind of market the local area is. However, you'll want to take certain factors such as the list price to sales price ratio, any seasonal issues that may arise, and the average number of days that homes in the area are on the market into consideration.

## Know the facts about the property and the seller

Not only will you need to know things about the property like how long it's been on the market, but it's good to know what the seller's motivation and priorities are. Why are they selling it?

What price do they want? Keep in mind that the seller may sell the house for a reasonable offer (even if it isn't the price they originally wanted to settle with). A seller may need money for something, or they might be making mortgage payments on another home and don't want to pay an additional one.

Also, the competition is something you want to keep any eye on. Because you might not be the only person interested in the property.

## Make your best offer on your first offer

You want to make the best offer possible at the outset. Keep in mind that the seller may counteroffer to ensure that you pay more. You may even offer a price higher than the seller expects. If you offer something that's $10,000 above the asking price compared to someone making one $5,000 above, then you might snag the property without the seller giving a counteroffer to the other.

Stay within the price of which you are pre-approved for. That way, you can make monthly payments at the new price (albeit a higher one at that). Also, don't make an offer that is above what the property could be appraised for.

## 7 Mistakes to Avoid

Now that you have a rough idea of how the offer process works, here are the mistakes that you need to avoid while making one:

### 1. Rejected for pre-approval of mortgage

If you cannot get pre-approved for a mortgage, that might put you at a disadvantage. Sellers will nine times out of ten favor those who are pre-approved for financing. That's because the pre-approval lets them know that they will have the money once the deal is done.

## 2. Bidding the pre-approved amount in its entirety

If the bank hands you a loan that's $450,000, resist the urge to make an offer that is the same amount. This could hurt you in the long-run should you go about doing this. Also, it will obliterate any breathing room that you'll have for negotiating.

The less you spend, the better off you'll be.

## 3. Not doing your research

This includes researching the market and the seller of the property. The more intel you have, the better prepared you'll be to make an offer. This research should go beyond the comparables and the price that it's listed for on the market.

As for the seller, if you have their names, do some research on them. Their social media profiles should give you a clue on the kind of people you are working with. If anything, don't be creepy or stalkerish.

Keep any intel you may have on them to yourself. But use it to help put together what may be the perfect offer that they cannot not refuse.

## 4. Lowball offers

Don't lowball the seller. If the property is worth $350,000, don't offer $250,000. If you do so, the seller will basically freeze you out and you blew it. Simple as that.

## 5. Too many contingencies

Having too many contingencies is the equivalent to jumping through too many hoops. And the more hoops that need to be jumped, the less likely the closing will be a success. Keep those contingencies to a minimum to ensure that the deal goes without a hitch.

What are contingencies? We're talking about things like home inspection, the ability to acquire financing, and so on. Don't make it more complex than it has to be.

## 6. Using the same agent as the seller

Three words: conflict of interest. The short answer to this problem: hire a buyer's agent. Remember the part where you should not work with dual agents?

This is reason number one why you should never ever deal with dual agents at all.

## 7. Allowing your emotions to get in the way

You might be in awe of the home's features. But don't let that get you to the point where you can buy it and have your budget busted after the fact. Get a buyer's agent who will not only keep their own emotions in check, but will make sure to keep yours in check as well.

Even if the home looks good inside and out and you love it to death, you may not always be on the winning end of the deal.

## Negotiating Your Way into The Best Deal That You Can Get

We'll be taking a look at ten negotiation strategies that can work to your advantage to ensure that you get the best deal possible. This is an important section that you want to make sure that you have in your arsenal with every deal you find yourself in. Some sellers will be reasonable while others may take a little work to finally budge.

With that said, let's take a look at the following strategies:

### 1. Know the seller's personality type

There are four different 'color coded' personality types for sellers: red, blue, green, and brown. Once you get a good idea of their personality type, it will give you an idea of how to approach them. Let's break down each personality type in detail:

- **Red:** These are people who may have their emotions on their sleeves. They are transparent and have nothing to hide. They usually field offers from people they know first before anyone else. They'll try to get to know you better (to the point where you and the seller address each other on a first name basis). Feel free to share common interests and passions.

- **Blue:** Sellers with this personality will usually have no clue about what they want. They are emotionally open and tend to share stories that are of heartbreak. They are loyal to the decision they make and put other people first before themselves. However, they can be jumpy and scare off easily. Take your time with them and lead them to an offer that they are comfortable with. Nine times out of ten, they're looking for someone who will define what they need for themselves.

- **Green:** This is someone who is all business. Unlike a red, they are not in the business of making friends. They care more about the numbers than personal lives. They want to keep their cards close and receive an offer as soon as possible. When dealing with this personality, ask what their end goals are as far as selling the property is concerned. Also, have them make a reasonable offer by asking them.

- **Brown:** Like the green, they are not looking to make friends with the buyer. However, they are more direct with their end goals and have little time for dilly-dallying. So, keep the relationship professional and be prompt. Also, give them a straight answer as to whether or not you can help them achieve the goals they set forth.

2. Be aware that the negotiation will be an uphill battle

Yes, there is money at stake. And there may also be emotional attachments to the property. Also, you want to be aware that the seller will have expectations that may be based on the market.

3. Focus on the win-win, not 'winner take all'

Negotiations and offers should not be about who wins and who loses. The goal here is to ensure that both sides come out with a win. The seller gets a good amount of money out of the deal and you have a property that you can rent out and generate income with.

This will allow the both of you to focus on the solutions rather than the issues. Don't make the process a war between you and the seller. You have your best interests at heart and so do they.

Meet in the middle and the both of you will find something that will be worth striking a deal.

## 4. Use an escalation clause

An escalation clause is something that you can use to ensure that you better position yourself to get the property when there are multiple offers. This includes making an offer above the market price, but not exceeding a specific price in particular. The highest written offer will be sent along with the acceptance to the respective agents involved with the buyer and seller.

## 5. Use the market value instead of the asking price

Depending on the market, you may want to use the market value as your starting offer as opposed to the asking price that the seller has set forth. So typically, you'll want to shoot for a price that is slightly lower than what the seller will likely accept.

Do not confuse this with lowballing them (which is offering them a price much lower than the asking price). They may accept the deal or come back with a counteroffer (while not scaring off what appears to be a strong buyer).

## 6. Be aware of the following tactics

One of the tactics to watch out for is nibbling. Nibbling may be something that a seller may not like. That's because the buyer will want to purchase the property while asking for something a little extra. However, the seller will mostly not accept because it will eat away at the profits (hence the term nibbling).

Another thing that buyers tend to do is known as the 'hot potato'. The buyer may not have enough money for some reason or may not qualify for purchasing it at such a price. The buyer will present a problem and will try to pass it onto the seller and make it their problem.

As a seller, you may want to stay sharp and not give the buyer any room. As a buyer, you'd be smart not to do these tactics.

## 7. Learn the basics of persuasion

There are six basic building blocks of persuasion: reciprocity, scarcity, authority, consistency, liking, and consensus. You'll want to persuade people to act in a certain way. You can add on something extra and that could put the seller in the position to do you a favor just for being good to them.

## 8. Embrace the 'no'

Needless to say, the word 'no' is going to be thrown around a lot. Whether it's you saying it or the seller, this is a good word that the both of you will be accustomed with. A 'no' can move the deal forward and that's when the negotiations will begin.

## 9. Learn what the seller needs from the deal

It's important that the needs of both parties should be met. That's why you need to know what they are before reaching a fair deal. Don't be afraid to ask these questions towards the seller or even the agent representing them. Get a backstory on the property including the number of kids they've raised or whether or not the property was an investment property (kind of like what you're looking for).

## 10. Meet the seller in person, if needed

Face to face meetings with the seller are important. Because you'll be able to tell whether or not they are authentic and serious about selling the property or if they are just giving you the runaround. Meeting them will give you a good idea to get to know them better and know the personality type of the seller.

Also, in-person meetings will help you stand out. It will put you in a more favorable position since other buyers may not be so keen to meet with the seller themselves.

## Counteroffers

A counteroffer is a conditional acceptance. It's the seller stating, 'I accept the offer on the condition that you agree to this and that'. You will face three options: either you accept the counteroffer, submit a counteroffer of your own, or walk away.

If you want to negotiate these counteroffers, it would be best to have your agent help you out. Your agent will get a good idea of what the seller wants and assist you in putting together a counteroffer of your own should you present one.

Also, you'll want to learn something known as 'quid pro quo' or 'something for something'. You can get something from a seller under the condition that you give something that they want. In a common situation, the seller will want to close the deal at a higher sales price.

They should give you something in return as part of the deal (hence something for something).

## Purchasing Below Market Value

Is it possible to purchase a property at a below market value price? The short answer: yes. However, there are a few types of properties that will allow you to purchase at such low prices.

Two of the most common properties are foreclosures and fixer-uppers. One of the biggest caveats of acquiring either of these properties is the need for extra cash. That's because there's a good chance that a lion's share of it will be going towards repairs and renovations.

The goal is obviously increasing the value of the property and selling it at a much higher price when the time comes. Or you can command a higher rental rate once everything is fixed up. Either way, purchasing BMV properties might be an easier route for you to take if you are new to real estate.

## Closing and Settling the Paperwork

Finally, it's closing time. Your offer has been accepted and it's time to make it official. You'll be reviewing a purchase agreement, which is a real estate contract that was arranged between you and the property seller.

Keep in mind that the purchase agreement should not be confused with the offer. The offer is a proposal with conditions that is used to buy the property. It is drafted by the agent of both the seller and the buyer.

The buyer will pay the agreed upon amount and the seller will transfer the deed of the property over to them. In the terms of the agreement, this includes the price, closing target date, offer expiration date, the money deposit amount (in earnest), and details regarding who will pay for the title insurance, inspections, and so on.

Also included are adjustments regarding property taxes, utilities, and other fees. Typically, it will be the responsibility of the buyer from this point forward to handle all the repairs and maintenance (although the seller may have done some repairs beforehand).

## Final Thoughts

Making sure that the deal is done before any repairs are being made is important. Yes, the seller may do some repairs ahead of time. However, it may be up to you to finish where they start.

After acquiring the property, it is all up to you to take good care of it. And, you'll want to consider adding value to the property in more than a few ways. Be sure to brainstorm a few ideas on how to make the property more valuable and appealing before setting a budget.

Remember, if any repairs or renovations need to be made, you'll want to make sure that your modifications will be all up to go so the place is habitable for a tenant.

# Chapter 7: Planning and Preparing Before the Fix

This chapter will cover the repair and maintenance of a rental property. Now that you have a property in your possession, the next thing you need to do is get it fixed up. For most properties that are in need of repairs, the valuation has no place to go but up.

However, there is one caveat. You have to put in the work to ensure the place is in better condition than it was when you bought it. We'll be discussing the condition of the rental property in addition to how you can add value to the property.

You'll have a battle plan to work with before you even get the repairs started. Of course, this will be a major project that will take a good amount of money to complete. That's why we'll be discussing how you can make a budget and why it's important to have one.

We'll also show you how to stick with it the best you can. We'll even weigh the pros and cons of fixing it yourself versus hiring professionals to do it for you. At the end of this chapter, you'll already have a decision made on who will get the job done.

We'll talk about how to set up a schedule based on the tasks that need to be done and go over the kind of paperwork that you need before any huge projects begin. Let's get our hands down and dirty and discuss what you need to do:

## What is the Condition of Your Rental Property?

To pick up where we left off in the last chapter, you should already have a good idea of what condition the rental property is in. At this point, you'll already know what needs to be fixed. Also, you'll know what needs to be upgraded such as appliances.

The more thorough and accurate the inspection was, the better you'll be able to know what kind of repairs and upgrades are needed.

## Adding Value to Rental Properties

There are various projects that you can do to add value to your rental properties. We won't delve into a lot of it since we'll be discussing more in the next chapter. But if you seem to have no idea how to increase the value, we've got you covered.

These are some suggestions, but if you want to get creative you are more than welcome to. After all, it's your property. You do what you gotta do.

Here are the suggestions that we recommend:

## Landscape your garden

To begin, we'll start from the outside. Nothing is more beautiful and inviting quite like a garden. You might have a green thumb and put something together to make the property look beautiful from the outside. Because of this, you may prefer a tenant to be someone who might have a green thumb.

They can take care of the garden for you because they care about the flowers and keeping them beautiful. On top of that, you can also increase the 'curb appeal' of your home. Neighbors and others passing through will see that your property will stand out better than the rest of the neighborhood.

Consider evergreen plants or even colorful flowers if you so choose.

## Go green

Believe it or not, we're not talking about gardening here. We're talking about energy efficiency. Think about it, if you go green, think of the utility expenses that you'll pay month after month.

You'll actually be spending LESS on utilities as an expense (regardless if it's you or the tenant). And that will definitely give your cash flow a bit of cushion. Plus, your tenants would save some money every month on utilities themselves if push came to shove.

So, going green is a win-win for both of you.

## Consider remodeling

Throughout your inspection, you might have considered the idea of remodeling a specific area of the house. It could be the kitchen, the bathroom, or any place else. No matter what, remodeling an area will considerably increase the home's value.

But if you have no clue on which area you want to remodel, the most popular choice is usually the kitchen. This will include replacing the cabinets, re-painting the walls, and even making a few upgrades on the appliances.

## Turn the garage into a little something

They say the garage is for cars and even storage space. But what if we just think outside of the box on how to use it? So, what would be a good way to use the garage while adding value at the same time?

You can convert it into an extra living space if you want to. And it could also mean that you can add a little extra income as well. This would be the perfect set up if your tenants were roommates as opposed to a family with a few kids.

## Building an extension to the property

You could add on to the currently existing property if you so choose. The real question is: what would be considered an extension? Would it be an extra bedroom?

What about a bathroom? What if you don't have a garage? Ah ha...you can build a garage and use it to convert it into extra living space.

Talk about a double whammy! That's killing two birds with one stone, if we do say so ourselves. But in all seriousness, if there is a way to build an extension then figure out how much it will be to get it built.

## Setting A Budget for The Fix

Stating the obvious: doing these projects to increase the value of your property will not come cheap. It never does. But you knew this right from the beginning.

Having a budget handy to get the repairs done from start to finish will be important. This is why it's recommended to accompany the home inspector during the inspection process to get a good idea of how much you'll need to spend (ballpark estimate).

Here's what we suggest for a budget, so you know what to spend money on:

## 1. The essentials

What constitutes as the essentials? These can include plumbing, heating, electrical, or anything that requires repairing, replacing, or upgrading. Also, you'll want to keep in mind that some states will have different laws in terms of repairs and whether or not you need some kind of guidelines you need to follow. Specifically, these are guidelines that meet the health and safety standards of a potential tenant.

## 2. Curb appeal

You might already have a good idea on what you want to do on the outside. So, something like a garden or the like might be what you want to consider. After all, at least 30 percent of tenants will consider curb appeal as one of their main factors in deciding whether or not they want to rent the property or not.

At the same time, about a quarter of tenants would be willing to repair some of the exterior of the property such as the fence, driveways or walls (at least for a reduction of rent if at all possible).

## 3. Vacancies

Needless to say, the property will be vacant for many weeks before there is a tenant that moves in. In the meantime, it should give you a good cover while you are fixing up the place. Keep in mind that there is no set timeframe as to when your first tenant will move in.

Also, you'll want to keep your eye out for any external events that take place. These include a change in mortgage interest rates or massive job losses in the area (like the closure of a large employer). When in doubt, budget low in this regard (but not too low to the point where you may be drowning in a sea of losses).

## 4. Building codes

Even before the hammer hits a nail or fire up any power tools, there's one thing you need to make yourself aware of. You'll want to get a building permit for your project. This can be done by going through your local government agency that handles these (typically code enforcement or the like).

Keep in mind that there are fees that vary, and you must follow the safety standards in accordance with the local ordinances.

## 5. The interior repairs

What are the repairs that are needed? Do the pipes need fixing? Does the roof need a little tender love and care?

How about repainting the walls? It's all up to you at this point. You can make notes during or even after the inspection.

These can be minor repairs or major, urgent repairs (depending on what the inspection has unveiled). Be sure to double-check what else needs to be repaired before doing any major projects.

### This repair budget should not be confused with your repair/maintenance reserves

Before moving further, this is a budget that is for initial repairs. This should not be confused with the amount of money you set off to the side every month regarding repairs and maintenance. Yes, things happen.

So as a reminder, don't forget to set off 10 percent of your total rent income that will be your repair and maintenance reserve.

## Fixing It Yourself or Hiring Professionals, Make Your Choice

Would you be willing to do the repairs yourself or would you get a professional to get the job done for you? We'll be taking a look at the pros and cons of each so you can choose which route is best for you.

Let's compare:

### The pros of doing it yourself

**It saves you money:** Clearly, without the use of a contractor you'll be able to get the work done yourself and save money that would otherwise go to a professional. Enough said.

**Perfect for small projects:** If the projects are small scale, then they are easy enough to do by yourself.

This includes painting the interior, installing linoleum or vinyl flooring, or even building a wood deck.

**They don't take a long time to do:** It depends on your daily schedule. You might have a work schedule and it might take a few days as opposed to a weekend. Regardless, the project itself won't take a ridiculous amount of time to do unless you allow it to happen.

## The cons of doing it yourself

**Not suitable for large projects:** Not only is tackling a large project solo a monumental task, but it's also unsafe to do. You could risk serious injury or even death depending on the project that needs to be done.

## The pros of hiring a professional

**Great for large projects:** Does the bathtub need to be replaced? Do you need hardwood or ceramic tile floors? Or what about replacement windows? This is where the professionals come in. There's a contractor for any large project you can think of.

**High-quality projects:** When it's professionally done, the quality will be way better compared to doing it yourself. Therefore, the repairs and renovations will last longer than usual. Years or decades likely.

**Quick to get approved for permits:** A contractor will quickly get approved for a local permit to work on a project on your property. Unlike doing it yourself, you may need to wait a bit or pay out of pocket. For contractors, it's just another business expense.

### The cons of hiring a professional

**It can be expensive:** Sure enough, professional contractors can be expensive. It will depend on the contractor and also the area they focus on. To help mitigate any unwanted costs, don't be afraid to shop around and ask for any recommendations. Again, your real estate network may also refer you to contractors (but they may not be the best decision due to affordability).

## Set a Realistic Schedule

Setting up a schedule for the whole entire project is a must. If the project will take days, make sure that the schedule focuses on that one specific area of the house. You cannot go all over the place for the entire week (i.e.: part of the kitchen one day, part of the bathroom the next, and so on).

You'll want to keep it simple and straightforward. How long will the project take by estimation? Schedule those days straightforward.

Once that part of the property is complete, move on with the other part that needs repairing. When should demolitions be scheduled? When will the repairs start?

To get a good idea of what a construction schedule looks like, check out this article and you'll see a couple examples of them.

## The Paperwork Involved for A Fix (In Case You Are Doing A Big Fix)

In the event of a big fix, you are going to need some of the following papers to ensure you are doing the job properly and legally. Let's take a look at what you need:

### Permits (Electric, Plumbing, Etc.)

If you are planning on doing any work regarding the plumbing and electricity, you may need a permit for it. Requirements may vary depending on the location you are in. If you are working on a property that is in a state that is different from yours, remember that you must adhere to the requirements in the property located in that state.

## Contract agreements

This will be an agreement between the contractor and the property owner. The terms and conditions set forth by the contractor will be laid out here.

## Statement of Work (SOW)

This piece of paper provides you with the scope of the project. This will determine the amount of work that will be needed.

## General conditions

This will provide you with the obligation and the rights on how the project should be executed. Included in the general conditions are what you can claim for overhead costs and your rights as a property owner.

## Special conditions

This is an extension of the general conditions if and when needed. The special conditions must be specific depending on the job or project. This is part of the paperwork that you need to pay special attention to if some conditions are included.

## Bills of Quantities

This will include a list of materials and trades that are included within the project. This is an optional part of the paperwork and the contractor can choose not to use it.

## Drawings/Mockups

These drawings or mockups are the most recent design of the project that you want done. These will also be due to the contractor prior to the beginning date for construction.

## Construction insurance

This will be useful in the event if something happens during a construction project. This may include mistakes being made, ill-fittings, and other issues that may arise while the work is being done.

## Construction schedule

As mentioned earlier, a construction schedule will be useful since it determines how and when the project will be completed. There may be a construction schedule needed for any multiple room projects. Make sure that there is a construction schedule for each room that you want remodeled or constructed.

# Final Thoughts

Before any repairs and renovations begin, it's better to plan them all out. This way, you'll want to decide what needs to be worked on and in a timely manner. Also, you want to make sure that you have the accurate budget to pull off the job.

You do have the choice to do it yourself. Yet, some larger projects may not be easy enough for one person to do all alone. If push comes to shove, be sure to contact a contractor that focuses on a certain area like kitchens, bathrooms, or residential remodeling or repairs.

The key here is to add more value to your rental property. This will help you command a higher rental rate for your tenants. At the same time, you can also sell the property at a higher price when the time comes.

# Chapter 8: Fixing Houses While Keeping in Mind That It's for Rental Properties

You managed to purchase a property that needs some fixing up. First off, congratulations. It might have been tough to get the deal done on your end...but here you are.

This chapter will focus on the repairs and renovations that could be needed in your new property (assuming it's some kind of fixer-upper). We'll also be focusing on similar tasks should you consider the idea of adding value to the property itself. Either way, we'll be covering various tasks including demolition, excavation, landscaping, and everything in between.

Some of the tasks that we'll be discussing in detail may be a do-it-yourself task or may require a professional contractor to get the job done. However, if you decide to travel the DIY route, we'll provide you with tips and guides on what you can do with certain projects such as remodeling the kitchen, changing the floors, and even adding additional square footage to your new property.

Keep in mind that this isn't your own home that you are working on. This is for a rental property that will help you generate income in the future. The more work you put in, the more valuable your property is going to be.

In turn, the more valuable the property, the more enticing it will be for a tenant. And you can generate plenty of income if you repeat this process with multiple properties. Now, we are getting into the fun stuff.

Let's start tearing stuff down, building it back up, and show you how to get the hard work done:

## Having Fun with Demolition

First and foremost, let's focus on demolition. Specifically, we'll be focusing on the interior as opposed to the outside of the property. Before moving any further, allow us to note the following:

***Safety notice:*** *During a demolition or any other project involving the repair and renovation of your properties, always wear the necessary protective gear to prevent serious injury or even death. These include safety glasses, hard hats, gloves, overalls, or any appropriate attire.*

Now that we have that safety message out of the way, let's talk specifics in terms of demolition. What will you plan on tearing down? Are you looking to tear down a wall, a complete room, or the entire interior?

Your choice will also mean higher costs. For example, if you are planning on tearing down one wall (without reconstruction), that will be low in cost. However, those costs go up when you want to demolish a room or the entire interior ($2,500 is the average for room demolition while the entire interior is estimated at $10,000).

For this reason, you want to consider your options in terms of what's staying up and what's going down. Keep in mind that different types of removal like tile, floor, wall and so on will be charged on a square foot basis. For example, floor removal could range from $2 to $5 per square foot.

Don't forget, there are labor costs that you want to factor in as well. Consider $20 an hour as an average starting point. The price range for interior demolition will run anywhere between $500 to $12,000 depending on how much needs to be torn down.

Before any demolition occurs, be sure to get a permit (if applicable). If you are planning on removing things off the property, get estimates from contractors or consider costs when done by yourself.

## How many dumpsters will I need?

Considering that you'll be disposing a lot of material, you're going to need dumpsters. How many you're going to need will depend on how much you're taking down. It will also depend on the kind of debris that you are throwing out. For example, if the house is 1,000 square feet and you have about 135 cubic yards of debris to remove, you'll need three and a half 40-yard dumpsters.

Keep in mind that the dumpster charges will depend on the weight of the debris that is being thrown out. So, consider talking to your local sanitation or waste management facilities and shop around for prices.

## What to dispose and what to recycle?

During the demolition process, you'll want to consider what you need to throw away in the dumpster and what needs to be recycled. Obviously, you'll want to dispose of materials like old or even rotting materials that may hurt the structural integrity. Harmful materials like asbestos must always be removed safely (and should also be done by professionals).

As for what needs to be recycled, there are more than 70 percent of building materials that can be recycled. These include but are not limited to the following: beams, doors, lumber, and windows. Also, you should consider recycling sinks, tubs, glass from windows, nails, and even copper pipes.

### Make sure everything is disconnected

Prior to demolition, it is important to make sure that the project is done safely. This includes disconnecting the electricity, sewage, gas, and water. Also, you want to close off the area, so no one steps on the property by complete accident and ends up in danger.

## Excavating an Area

This should not be something you do if there are minor repairs that need to be done around the house. However, there are instances where excavating is necessary. Such examples include landscaping and also adding a swimming pool with the intent to increase the value of the property.

Excavation uses specialized machinery that shifts the earth, rocks, and other underground obstacles that need to be removed prior to construction. Nine times out of ten, a professional will handle this (unless you have access to excavation equipment). Once again, you should check to see if you have any licenses or permits to do an excavation (or consult a contractor that does have the proper approval).

Before any excavation can be done, there's always the precaution of surveying the area. You'll want to know exactly where excavation and construction will be done. Keep in mind that surveying the area will be beneficial since there is no guarantee that blueprints will be accurate for safe digging.

On top of that, you'll want to reduce the number of potential problems as much as possible. And you also want to reduce any community downtime that may arise due to an excavation project. Also, be sure to have the soil professionally tested before any construction occurs.

## Landscaping

If you want to increase the curb appeal and the overall value of the property from the outside, consider landscaping. As a newbie to real estate, you don't need to go all out. You want landscaping projects to be as low-maintenance as possible.

Plus, if a tenant wants to do landscaping themselves, you don't want to put them in a position where they have to put in a lot of work. Especially when all they want to do is relax. So, don't pressure them into doing so much.

In this section, we're going to talk about some of the basics of low maintenance landscaping. We'll also discuss some of the 'do's and don'ts'.

## Low maintenance landscaping ideas

As mentioned before, landscaping your property doesn't have to be a lot of work. You want to keep it as simple and low maintenance as possible. So, let's give you a few ideas to work with:

- **Weed control:** Instead of pulling weeds, consider applying a protective weed barrier to ensure that they are not growing all over the place (and at an alarming rate). Applying mulch to your yard will also keep the weeds at bay as well.

- **Consider hardscaping:** If you want to lessen the maintenance level as much as possible, hardscaping may be an excellent solution. You can remove plants on the property and replace it with walkways, patios, or borders. The less surface area containing plants, the better.

- **Add a small garden:** This is completely optional. But it would make the home a lot more attractive to tenants and even the neighbors. As long as the garden is tended to on a regular basis by you or the tenant, then it will certainly be an excellent landscaping addition.

## The 'Do's' and 'Don'ts' of Landscaping

Let's take a look at some of the things you should and shouldn't do if you are landscaping the property:

### DO:

- **Keep a neutral theme:** A neutral theme should be fine. Leave the personalization up to the tenant.

- **Consider plants or shrubs that are native/local:** If you are planning on adding some plants or shrubs, make sure they are native to your local area. This will help you save money and preserve biodiversity in the process. On top of that, it won't require a lot of maintenance as well.

- **Make shade a priority:** In the summertime, too much sun can be a bad thing. Especially when it comes to certain plants. Therefore, they'll need plenty of shade to counteract the amount of sun they're getting every day. Pay attention to the plant labels so you know how much sun a specific plant needs.

DON'T:

- **Overdevelop the yard:** Quality matters. Not the quantity. So, don't go overboard in terms of the pavement or hardscaping.

- **Don't personalize it:** To tie in with keeping a neutral theme, don't personalize the landscaping to your liking. Remember, this is a rental property that you own. It's not your primary residence.

- **Restrict yourself:** Even with planting new plants, don't feel like you're restricted to your current layout. You can move and replace plants if need be and set them up in different areas of the property. Don't be afraid to play around a bit rather than feel like the plants need to stay in a specific area.

## Replacing or Repairing the Roof

During your inspection, the roof should have been inspected thoroughly along with the rest of the property. If there are any holes or flaws, they need to be repaired as soon as possible. Replacing the roof in its entirety can also be an option.

Water leakage from the roof due to rain or snow may lead to water damage (which leads to mold growth). And that alone will be a recipe for disaster if left unchecked. One thing to be aware of is if the roof needs work, then that's a project that needs to be left up to the professionals.

## Should I repair or replace the roof?

Of course, there's a difference between repairing the roof and replacing it. So, when is a good time to do either or? Let's take a look first at when repairing the roof should be the best option:

### When to repair:

- **If there are leaks around the pipe boot or chimney**
- **Nail pops**
- **Damage from trees**
- **Weather damage**
- **Shrinkage**
- **Splitting**
- **Poor install**

- **Cracking or blistering**
- **Granule loss**
- **Punctures or holes**
- **Ventilation issues**

Keep in mind that repairing the roof will help you save a ton of money compared to replacing it all together. On top of that, you'll also be expanding the longevity of the roof. Not to mention, it will increase the curb appeal.

However, matching shingle colors is one of the greatest challenges for repairing a roof because they may be hard to come by.

### When to replace:

- **If the roof is worn**
- **The roof is too old**
- **Major vulnerability to future damage**

Replacing the roof will likely occur if it's wearing or showing signs of advanced age. Also, major vulnerabilities that are exposed will also lead to damage in the future. The best preventative measure at that point would be to replace the roof.

When replacing a roof, you'll have peace of mind knowing that a crisis will be averted. Yet, roof replacements can be noisy and even costly.

## Adding Square Footage

One of the best ways to add value to your property is adding more square footage. We'll be taking a look at some of the best ways to do that so you have a good idea of what you can build should you want to add more space beyond the current layout.

When adding square footage, it's also possible to save money in the process. Let's take a look at some ideas on how to add square footage to your rental property

### 1. Build into the backyard

The backyard is usually a great place where you can add more square footage. This includes a patio or even expanding a room like a kitchen or a dining room. Not only does this give you the opportunity to expand, but a little bit of extra square footage in this manner can definitely help with bumping up the rent.

## 2. Build a greenhouse

A greenhouse is a nice way to add more square footage. At the same time, it will also give you plenty of space to grow a garden on the inside. You'll want to make sure that the greenhouse is properly equipped with the right kind of drainage system.

You'll also want to use the proper materials that will provide your plants with the appropriate climate. And finally, be sure that your greenhouse is in compliance with any HOA rule (if such are applicable).

## 3. Think big...or small

Whether it's adding another level or adding a small patio to the back yard, a nice sized expansion might be just what you need to give your property a little more square footage (and extra value in the process). You can build a small deck, a large pavilion in the backyard, or add another level to the home with new rooms.

When adding another level, this gives you a good opportunity to add more bedrooms or bathrooms to the property. That will give you plenty of opportunities to build upgraded bathrooms and bedrooms right from the start. The better they look, the more valuable your property is.

## Changing Floors

Changing the floors can be done by yourself or a professional. The way it works is that the old flooring will need to be lifted (depending on the material). And in its place, a new floor will be installed. However, flooring comes in different materials. So, the installation process will differ. Also, it's important to consider which type of flooring is best.

It wouldn't make a lot of sense if you installed a carpet in the kitchen and linoleum in the living room, would it? Of course not.

### The Dos and Don'ts of Flooring

Yes, there are some flooring 'dos' and 'don'ts'. And it's important that you follow these when you are doing the project yourself. Let's take a look at the 'Do's" first:

#### DO:

- **Know your budget:** This cannot be said clear enough. You'll want to find the best flooring that you can afford in terms of quality and style. Don't have your heart set on a specific type of flooring only to find out it is double your budget.

- **Know your flooring needs:** Your needs will far outweigh your dreams and wants for flooring. Think about it: would it be smart to put a hardwood floor in an area that will always get dirty? Probably not. But you want something that is durable and easy to clean, regardless of where it is in your house.

- **Know which floor is best for each room:** There's always a natural match for floors and the appropriate rooms. For example, a carpet would go well in a bedroom but never a bathroom. Or a tile floor would go well in a warmer room of the house, not a colder one. Get the idea?

DON'T:

- **Be afraid to ask the professionals:** You don't have to be a flooring expert to do a DIY project. But if you are worried about doing it wrong, then consider asking the professionals for advice. Alternatively, you can hire professional flooring experts to do the job for you.

- **Install a floor where it might not be appropriate:** A hardwood floor would be nice in just about any part of the house. However, it would not be wise to install it in a high traffic area like a doorway. Also, it might be weird just installing a carpet in a place where you typically install linoleum or vinyl.

## What floors to consider

Choosing floors can be a hassle. But if you know which flooring will work best (and where to install it), you should be in good shape. Let's take a look at the flooring options you have:

### Carpets

Carpets are excellent for insulation and will help reduce energy bills. It will also reduce a lot of noise as well. These are great for bedrooms or even upper-level rooms. They will not work well in bathrooms, basements, entryways, hallways, or kitchens.

### Tile

These are available in stone, porcelain, or ceramic. They are durable, water resistant, and can be cost effective. But the cleaning and maintenance can be a real pain.

You can install these in basements, bathrooms, kitchens, or rooms that are humid in climate. If your property is located in a colder climate, avoid installing them altogether.

### Hardwood

Hardwood floors come in different species of wood. Cut into planks, these are nailed over the sub-floor. Easy to clean and has a long lifespan, these floors will be best for bedrooms, dining rooms, living rooms, or a home office.

These hardwood floors won't fare well in bathrooms since they are susceptible to water damage. These floors may be difficult to install. So, you may want to consider a professional installation if possible.

### Laminate

This will be a good option if hardwood is out of your price range. And it can be much easier to install as well. This will go great in dining rooms, bedrooms, living rooms, or offices.

Like hardwood floors, laminate is not appropriate to install in bathrooms because of possible water damage. At the same time, laminate should not be installed in kitchens or basements.

### Vinyl

Vinyl is water resistant, cost effective, and easy to install. This kind of flooring is perfect for the do-it-yourselfer. These will usually go nicely in bathrooms or kitchens.

However, you may want to be aware that this floor type is not durable and may be susceptible to mold or mildew if enough moisture gets underneath it.

### Linoleum

If you are looking for something that is environmentally friendly, linoleum might be the best choice. It's affordable, easy to install, and easy to clean. Only install these in dining rooms and kitchens.

One major con to be aware of is that it can be prone to dents and tears.

## Remodeling the Kitchen

The kitchen is where the magic happens in the culinary sense. While your tenant may not be a professional chef, they will love seeing a kitchen that is brand new and very stylish. If you truly want to give your property a bump up in value, one of the best ways to go about doing it is remodeling the kitchen.

When remodeling the kitchen, most of the work goes into removing and replacing the appliances like the refrigerator, the stove and oven, and even the kitchen sink. This will depend on what you're planning to do.

With every good remodeling project, you want to put together a budget, so you'll know how much you're spending. You can compare things like refinishing the cabinets versus replacing them or choosing one type of countertop over the other. Most of the time, repairing and remodeling will always be more cost effective than replacing things.

## Kitchen remodeling tips that will save you money

Don't get us wrong. But kitchen remodeling does not come cheap. However, you can soften the blow of your wallet.

These tips below will show you how to go about saving money while making your kitchen look brand spanking new. Let's take a look:

## 1. Do it yourself

If you want to save money, doing it yourself is the best option. That means no contractors or professionals throughout the entire project. However, the one caveat is that if this is your first time remodeling the kitchen, you may have no choice but to hire a contractor.

But for subsequent properties (should you acquire them), this will be the best possible option.

## 2. Get down and dirty

Get a sledgehammer and get to work. It might be fun smashing the crap out of an old kitchen. Plus, it pays to do that since you'll be saving money. Remember to get the right permits to use a dumpster (if applicable), do your demo during the day, and notify your neighbors ahead of time for any noises and the like.

## 3. Get multiple bids and negotiate

There can't be one general contractor in your area that is interested in a project. There may be several others. Get a list of contractors that you're considering and start negotiating with them.

Do not accept the first offer whether it's the lowest or not. Get an offer that will give you the best quality that you can afford. Never skimp on quality just because you want to save a few dollars.

You might get a beautiful countertop that usually is a lot in value for a fair price just because you asked.

## 4. Get your appliances during special holidays

If you want to get a good deal on appliances, there is no better time to get them than during a holiday sale. Memorial Day, the 4th of July, etc. there will be special sales. Also, the prices of appliances like refrigerators, stove and oven sets, and others will be at their lowest price.

For example, refrigerator models from various brands will dip down at around the 4th of July and around Black Friday/Cyber Monday. However, the best time to do remodeling is the former. That's because in the winter months, you'll lose a lot more money due to vacancies.

Also, you'd be remiss if you didn't get your appliance from major stores like Home Depot, Best Buy, or even Lowe's.

## 5. Reuse materials if need be

We're tempted to throw a lot of stuff away during a remodeling. But the best way to save money is to find out which materials can be reused and go down that road. Instead of throwing materials away, you can consider repainting or refacing kitchen cabinets.

Another thing to reuse is light fixtures. So long as they are in good condition and not too old, you can keep them around longer rather than replace them.

## 6. Time your renovations just right

The timing of your renovation should not conflict with peak rental seasons. So, it would be ideal to start your renovations in the spring and have them wrapped up right around the summertime or thereabouts.

If there is a tenant that wants to get out of a lease early and you're planning on doing some property renovation, you can allow it. This way, that will grant them their release while fulfilling your interest in renovating the property and getting more in rent from the next tenant. Talk about a win-win.

### 7. Consider installing an island counter

An island counter would be perfect for a kitchen. It would be the perfect place to prepare food or even install a dishwasher when there is no other place to install it. Plus, it would make a great centerpiece for any renewed kitchen.

### 8. Give your tenants a gift

Once you have a new tenant that is about to move into the rental property, leave them a nice welcoming gift for the kitchen. This can include a kitchen set, cleaning products, and so much more. This will help them save money while you help jumpstart what will be a trusting relationship between you and them.

## Expanding Closet Space

Having a closet and storage space might just come in handy. And you might have tenants who hate the idea of having to deal with a lot of clutter. But why not give them a little more than they want?

Expanding closet space might be a good idea. Because your tenants may have stuff that they want to store away. They may even have a lot of clothes or linens.

But how can it be done on a tight budget? Let's take a look at a few tips:

- **Install central shelves or lazy susans:** If you want to maximize storage in a kitchen, you can consider installing central shelves on an island or install lazy susans in a corner cabinet. This will not only save you plenty of space, but it will also make your rental property look even better.

- **Bathroom cabinets:** You can build a bathroom cabinet that can be attached to the tub or shower. Or you can install a medicine cabinet with a mirror for more space. Giving your tenants more options to keep things organized will be way better than having them fend for themselves.

- **Closets:** One of the issues with closets is that they have wasted space. So why not consider the idea of installing an organizing system to ensure that the space is used to your advantage? For a master bedroom, consider the idea of expanding space for a walk-in closet. That will give tenants the ultimate opportunity of privacy and organization all in one space.

## Painting It with New Colors

Painting the property isn't too difficult. But there are some challenges that present itself such as choosing the right colors. Will you need to paint the interior or the exterior?

Or will it have to be both? Either way, the goal with painting your property is to improve the overall value while giving it a boost in curb appeal. If you are planning on doing some repainting, let's discuss some of the things you'll want to do before you dip the brush in the bucket.

### Exterior painting

First and foremost, you want to check to see if the exterior is in good shape. During your inspection, here's what you need to look for:

- **Is the paint bubbling, peeling, or chipping?**
- **Is the caulking cracked?**
- **Is the stucco damaged?**

- **Are the current colors fading?**

If you see any positive signs of this, that's when you know that the exterior will need to be painted. You can do this by yourself or have a professional contractor do it for you. Depending on your needs and your budget, choose the best option that's right for you.

### How often should exteriors be painted?

The short answer: it depends on the material. Let's take a look at the different materials and how often you may need to paint them:

- **Brick:** Every 10 to 12 years
- **Aluminum siding:** 6 years
- **Wood siding:** 5 to 7 years
- **Stucco:** 6 to 8 years

## Choosing the right type of paint and colors

Another one of the more challenging things about painting your property is choosing the colors. Or maybe even the type of paint. Whether you are painting the interior, exterior, or both you'll want to choose the right kind of paint based on your needs rather than wants.

Here are some tips that you should follow:

## Choosing the right colors

When it comes to choosing the right colors, it's important that you steer clear from bright colors, camouflage, or even colors that resemble national flags. The reason why is because they do not have mass appeal and it might turn off tenants.

This means you'll have to go with an attractive, but neutral color. Consider choosing one of the following colors: grey, beige, off-white, or tan.

## Choosing the right type of paint

There are five different types of paint finishes. You'll want to choose the right one depending on the interior materials or the room type. Here are the options for finishes and what makes them great:

**Flat or matte:** This finish is non-reflective and will conceal plenty of surface flaws. This is great when you want to fill cracks and other imperfections. Use this kind of paint for low traffic areas of your home such as bedrooms.

**Eggshell:** It's soft and velvety. But it isn't glossy. This will work well in rooms that have a medium amount of traffic like living areas, sunrooms, even bathrooms. Compared to flat finishes, this will hold up a lot better.

**Satin:** This has a bit more shine than eggshell. And it can be used for medium to high traffic areas of the property such as entryways and living areas. These can fare better in kitchens because of the amount of moisture that can be produced from there. This kind of paint is easy to maintain and may show application flaws after the fact.

**Semi-gloss:** This is by far one of the most durable finishes. And it's easier to wash should stains be present. This is perfect for medium to high traffic locations in your property. And it will work great with most surfaces such as woodwork, moldings, trims, doors, and windows (among others).

**Hi-gloss:** The most durable and washable paint of them all. This will be perfect for high-use surfaces.

## DIY vs a professional: When to choose?

If you want to save money, the clear option is to do the painting yourself. However, if you are planning on painting the exterior of the property, you may want to consider a professional since the project will be a bit more complex.

Interior paint jobs are mostly done by do-it-yourselfers. So, if you want to make it easier on yourself, consider doing the inside of the property (assuming the exterior is in good shape).

## Other Repairs and Upgrades That You Should Consider

By now, you already may have had some ideas on what needs to be repaired and upgraded. There might have been a laundry list that you put together during the initial pre-offer inspection. Now would be a good time to double check what else is needed?

For example, does the plumbing need repairing or upgrading? How are the pipes looking? Is the shower, sink, and toilet working well?

Also, what could you do to improve the curb appeal of the property? And how can you improve it while on a tight budget? Remember, simplicity is what you want so you don't let it eat into your cash reserves.

With that said, let's take a look at some ideas that you should at least consider:

- **Paint the front door:** Is the color boring? Is it not that appealing from the outside? Then consider the idea of painting it a color that will match the exterior nicely. White will usually match well with any color.

- **Replace the mailbox:** Is the mailbox falling apart? If so, replace it.

- **Make your street numbers stand out:** If the exterior has no street numbers, get them. Make sure they stand out nicely. Make it fresh and modern. It takes 15 minutes to install and no more than $15.

- **Improve the garage doors:** You can paint them, fix them up, or install materials to make it look more appealing. A tenant may use the garage door as an indicator of how the rest of the property will look.

- **Light up your front path:** Why depend on a single lamp post or a floodlight? Consider lighting up your front path like a runway using solar-powered lights or spotlights. Add a few of them in your garden beds as well.

## Preparing the Property

Whether it's a showing or prior to moving in, you'll need to prepare the property, so it looks like things are in working order and clean. This means spending time checking everything around the property. Here are some tips that you need to follow in order to prep the property:

## Make sure everything is working

Make sure that the phone and Internet connections are in working order. Next, test the heating and cooling systems to ensure that they are working properly and warming or cooling the property correctly. Also, check the locks to ensure that they secure the doors properly.

Since privacy is important, see if you have curtains that cover the windows. Alternatively, you can use blinds or shades. Lastly, check to see if the smoke detectors are installed and working.

## Clean the place if needed

Everything should be spotless. The floors should be vacuumed, the sinks, toilets, kitchen counters, and everything else dusted and wiped down. Also, check to see if corners are free from cobwebs.

Make sure that the outside is presentable. The gutters should be cleaned. The grass should be mowed (and no weeds are included).

### Make small repairs if needed

If there are broken lights, tiles, windows, and latches, fix them as soon as possible. These repairs should take anywhere between a few minutes to a few hours (depending on what needs to be repaired).

## Final Thoughts

Fixing up properties for the purpose of increasing the value of your rental properties will be one of the smartest things you do. Especially if your goal is to get a tenant onto the property and collect rent from it.

Demolition may be needed if you need to do some remodeling projects such as the bathroom or the kitchen. Just make sure that you have the right kind of paperwork to get it done. It might also be a fun do it yourself project if you get the work done safely.

Also, keep in mind the kind of flooring that you'll need for each room in your property. Remember that some types of flooring will only be fitting for some rooms, but not all of them. You really don't want to put a carpet in the bathroom or a tile floor in the bedroom, no?

If needed, you can consider the idea of repainting some rooms of the property (or even the outside if you must). Remember to choose neutral colors that will stand out and make the place look nice. There are projects that can be done as a DIY project while others may require a professional to get it done.

However, if you are planning on getting a professional to do the projects for you, keep in mind how much money you have in your budget. Sometimes, doing it yourself is the best route so you can save money.

Lastly, be sure that everything is in good shape prior to presenting the property to potential tenants. Make sure everything is clean, working properly, and your presentations will go forward without any issue.

# Chapter 9: What You Need to Know and Do to Finally Start Renting

By now, you have reached the point where your rental property is ready to go. You're finally ready to start renting it out to your first tenant. This chapter will be focused on what you need to do prior to fulfilling your vacancies.

We'll be answering the question of how much you should charge for rent? Also, you need to be aware that your rental property vacancies won't fill themselves. So, it is important to know how to market and advertise (without being a marketing wizard).

You'll learn how to choose the right tenants and do so while abiding to the Fair Housing Act. When you have whittled it down to the final candidates, you'll want to present the property to them, so they know what the property looks like and what they'll be paying for.

People will start applying to fulfill your vacancies. And it will be up to you on how to fulfill them. We'll also discuss rental contracts and how they work.

Lastly, we'll also discuss what to do next when you have chosen a tenant and they finally move in. This is a big step in your real estate investing journey. And you probably could not be more excited. Now, let's dive right in and get to the good stuff:

## How Much Should You Charge for Rent?

Before moving any further, let's give you a brief reminder: you'll want to choose a rental rate that will keep your cash flow in the green rather than operating at a loss. Also, you want to keep in mind of the expenses that you will be paying every month for the property itself. So how much should you charge exactly?

It will depend on several factors. For one, there's the location. You could be closer to the downtown area and charge a high enough rental fee because of its walkability, close proximity to points of interest and more. Whereas, if you're in the suburbs, the rent may be lower.

By now, you should have a good idea of what the average rental rate is for an area. However, if you are in a highly populated city, your rent may be more expensive compared to lesser populated areas (Ex: Los Angeles will command higher rates than properties in Cleveland).

If you live in states like Oregon, New York, California, District of Columbia, New Jersey, or Maryland, you'll want to be aware that there are rent control laws. This means you can dictate how much you can charge and how much you can increase in the future.

Also, you can follow what is known as the '1 percent rule'. This will allow you to take the property's value and charge 1 percent of it as rent. For example, if the property you have purchased is $250,000, then one percent is $2,500.

## Security deposits explained

Security deposits are an amount of money (which typically is a month's rent). This is something the tenant will pay for on top of the first month's rent. This will be used to cover any damages and repairs that the tenant is responsible for.

If a tenant moves out, they can have the security deposit returned in its entirety or partially depending on any damages that have been incurred. Also, keep in mind that there may be laws that can determine whether or not security deposits will be used in certain situations. So be sure to remind the tenant to take good care of the property or risk losing their deposit or at least part of it.

## Start Advertising

As we've said early on, a tenant just cannot waltz into your rental property and plant their stake there. Nor will a vacancy fulfill itself. So, it's time to start advertising your property.

Advertising addresses a problem (someone is looking for a place to live). And you have the solution, (your rental property). However, in some forms of advertising, you'll need to exclude certain types of tenants like those who have a bad credit history, pay their rent late, or anything that may cause certain problems for you.

What are some of the best ways to advertise your rental properties? Let's take a look at a few places where you can start:

- **Online ads and listings:** We live in an age where online ads like Facebook and Google are geocentric to the point where you can only show it to people who live near a certain area. The more laser focused it is on a certain area, the better it will perform. But it's not always a guarantee that you may get a ton of leads. But it's focused on a certain age group, gender, and the like. Also, you can depend on websites like Apartments.com, Craigslist or the like.

- **Classified ads:** Yes, landlords still like to go old school. So, you can post a classified ad in the local newspapers or certain guides that offer 'Buy, Sell, or Trade-Ins'. Keep in mind that ads of specific spaces will be charged by space. Meaning a small ad will be financially sound compared to a larger space ad that commands a higher rate.

- **Flyers:** Flyers with photos of the property will usually get a bunch of eyeballs. You can place these flyers in high traffic areas like community bulletin boards, supermarkets, laundromats, college campuses, and more. Make sure the photos are clear, colorful, and gives someone the exact details of what the property looks like.

As for what to include in your advertising, it's important to eliminate the potential 'problem tenants'. Speaking of which, we'll be talking more in depth about them right now.

## Pick Your Tenants, Never Randomly Accept or Choose One

It would be a mistake to randomly draw a name out of the hat and give that person your rental property. If you need to choose the right tenant, you'll need to be thorough. For this reason, you'll need to do the following when performing a background check:

- **Credit history:** The better someone's credit history is, the more likely they'll pay on time and be financially stable. There may be a certain credit score that will be considered a cut-off point where you can automatically reject applicants. Hey, it's kind of the same as applying for a loan. Bad credit? Instant rejection.

- **Criminal history:** Your rental property may be in a neighborhood that is considered safe. However, you want to pay special attention to this section. And you want to double check if your applicants are telling the truth. There may be certain crimes that will automatically disqualify them from renting from you (i.e. -- domestic violence, drug crimes, sex crimes, etc.)

- **Rental history:** This will give you a good idea of whether or not they'll pay on time or if they're going to be a good tenant to deal with. Rental history will give you a list of references (such as past landlords) so you can confirm if they are a good person or someone who can frustrate you.

- **Employment History:** Can the tenant hold down a stable job? How long have they been with their current employer? This will be good indicators that they will be able to pay you for as long as the lease is intact.

To note, you have the choice to choose the applicants yourself or go through a property management firm that can handle all that heavy lifting. It can be a daunting task, but you'll need to use your better judgement here in terms of who should occupy your rental property. You want them to be someone that you can trust, not someone who is going to be difficult to deal with for as long as possible.

You may face difficult decisions in choosing a tenant because they might be considered 'model tenants'. But at the end of the day, someone is going to be moving into your property.

## Be Mindful of The Fair Housing Act

The Fair Housing Act was a law that was established in 1968. This law was created to limit any discrimination practices that involves housing. This was intended to give Americans an equal opportunity whenever they are looking for a place to live without the fear of being discriminated against.

As a landlord, it is up to you to give applicants a fair chance. Whether they are a minority, someone who is LGBT, or a non-citizen of the United States, it is incumbent upon you to give them consideration if they apply. They should not be automatically disqualified because of their race, orientation, or the like.

Those protected by the Fair Housing Act are based on the following factors:

- Color
- Disability
- Family status
- Nationality (including foreign nationals)
- Race
- Religion
- Gender

While sexual orientation is not one of the factors, we encourage you to consider going through the selection process as if it were. They should be treated and looked at the same way in terms of how they qualify. Focus on their credit history, rental history, and the other factors listed in the previous section.

If you are consistent with the screening process, this could protect you from any potential accusations of discrimination. One rule of thumb is to assume that everyone is working for the Department of Housing and Urban Development (or HUD). Treat everyone with respect and dignity and perform the regular qualification checks as usual.

## Presenting the Property to Possible Tenants

If you have whittled your list down to some of the last few candidates, it's time to show them the property. This may be something to include in your tenant selection process for a couple of good reasons. For one, you may have a potential tenant that might not like something about the property itself (like the paint color of all things or lack of walkability). Depending on the tenants, you can show them relevant areas of the property. For example, if the tenants are a family of four, you can show them the bedrooms where the kids will sleep. If it's a young married couple, then you can show them some of the features like the kitchen and living room space where they can entertain guests and have dinner parties.

### Common questions that tenants ask

During the showing, expect the tenants to be asking you some questions. These are common questions to which you will have answers on the fly. Your answers may be a 'make or break' deal for potential tenants.

Let's take a look at some of those questions:

## 'Do you allow pets?'

If you allow pets, explain what kind of pets are allowed. Also, you'll want to mention a pet fee if you choose to implement one. And you'll want to explain how it's charged.

Some landlords charge a flat fee or based on the pet's size. A tenant with a chihuahua would pay a lesser fee than someone with a husky. However, this may depend on the type of rental property.

Also, keep in mind that if the tenant has pets, you may command a higher rate to cover any pet related damages. If you do not want pets on the property, say so. Some potential tenants would never give up their pets just for the sake of moving into a property.

## 'Can I pay ahead up front and move in as soon as possible?'

This may sound like a good idea for both the landlord and tenant. However, this might be more of a red flag. Why is that?

This could be a sign that something may be negatively affecting the tenant on their end at some point in the near future. And they'll use this tactic to persuade the landlord to take more cash than usual. But this is a risky move that may constrict your cash flow rather than help it.

On top of that, the tenant may cause problems to the point where you evict them. And prepaid rent will make the situation more difficult. At this point, you should state that you do not accept prepaid rent.

If someone says that they are in a hurry and asks to pay the rent and move in the same day, the answer should be 'no'. They have to go through the application process like everyone else. Plus, it won't be fair to anyone who may want to see the property other than that prospective tenant.

## 'Will you consider a short-term lease?'

This will depend on the property you own. You may have apartment buildings that accept short-term lease tenants (or month by month). However, some of your properties will have long-term leases like apartments or single-family properties.

If you require a long-term lease, state that the lease minimum is 12 months, but recommend that if they want to stay longer than that, they can. If you do have vacancies that involve short-term leases, do not be afraid to make those recommendations to the potential tenant.

## 'Are you the owner?'

While you do own the property per se, it would be wise to address yourself as the 'property manager' instead. However, you are welcome to say that you are the owner as you so choose.

## 'Can my due date be the x?'

The short answer: no. It should be the first of every month. No ifs, ands, or buts. Moving on.

## 'I want my mom/sister/girlfriend/boyfriend to live with me, but is it OK if they are not on the lease?'

Another question with a short answer: no. The reason being is that if the tenant leaves and the other person still resides on the property, they are not technically a legal tenant. Therefore, you'll need to let prospective tenants know that anyone over the age of 18 must fill out an application, pass the screening requirements and be on the lease. No exceptions.

## What to Do When People Start Applying

Once you have tenants interested in applying, they'll do it using a regular paper form or online (depending on which will be easier for both you and the applicant). Also, you want to be clear on whether or not there are application fees.

During the application process, you want to require that tenants procure a copy of any identification including a driver's license, state identification, or a passport. Anything with their photo on it will be a plus.

If the application is all digital, you'll want them to send scanned copies of their ID. From there, you or the property management company that you hire will screen each application. What should be included in the application besides identification:

**Here are some things to include in your rental application:**

- **Photo ID**
- **Name**
- **Address**
- **Phone number**
- **Email**

- **Employment and income information**
- **Past addresses**
- **Pets (if any)**
- **Background information**
- **Rental history (and landlord references)**
- **Personal and professional references**
- **Emergency contacts**
- **Credit checks**

Aside from this information, you want to make sure that they are going to be reliable tenants that pay on time. As such, you can request their previous W2 or pay stubs dating back to a previous time period. Also, you'll want to ask if there are any additional tenants over the age of 18 (in this case, you may require them to fill out an application as well).

## When should you approve an applicant?

So, when is a good opportunity to approve an applicant? Consider the following:

- If they have good to excellent credit

- No felonies on their criminal record
- No bankruptcies or evictions
- Favorable responses from professional, personal, and landlord references
- Meet's any pet criteria

Keep in mind that they can be rejected if they do not meet some of the requirements listed above. However, if you have found someone with a better application, be sure to inform them in the best way possible.

While it's not considered an outright rejection, sometimes you have to swallow hard and make tough decisions. However, be sure to keep them in mind while they are still looking for a place. You may have another property that might better suit them than the original.

## How Do Rental Contracts Work?

Rental contracts are written agreements that will be signed by both you and the tenant. There are two kinds of contracts that you can offer depending on the property: month-by-month or lease agreements.

## Rental agreement

A rental agreement (or month-by-month) is perfect for short-term leases. If you have apartments that accept tenants on a month-by-month basis, these rental agreements can be renewed every month or can be allowed to expire.

A rental agreement can also be modified every month. A tenant and you will discuss any changes if need be.

## Lease agreement

Lease agreements will focus on the long term. At minimal, you'll be looking at 12 months. However, some tenants may be willing to stay on at least longer than that.

After the old lease has expired, you can consider changing the terms. However, the tenant may not agree to the changes and may decide to not renew. So, consider talking about possible changes to the lease before the old one expires.

## What's included in an agreement?

The following is included in a rental or lease agreement:

- **Tenants who are residing on the property (over the age of 18)**
- **The term of the tenancy (month-by-month or lease length)**
- **Rental rate plus security deposit**
- **Whether or not pets are allowed**
- **The responsibilities of the tenant in terms of utilities**
- **Permission for the landlord to access the property for repairs, maintenance, and inspections.**
- **Additional rules of the tenancy**
- **Damage policy**
- **Signatures (NOTE: The tenant must sign first before you do! Keep a copy for your records and encourage the tenant to keep a copy as well)**

## When A Tenant Moves In

When a tenant moves in, you'll want to do one final inspection of the property before moving day arrives. It's also important to welcome them to their new home and cover as many bases as possible as far as what they need to know about their property and what actions they need to take going forward.

Here are some tips on what to do when your tenant moves in:

- **Provide them with your contact information:** Communication between you and the tenant is key. You want to encourage them to keep in touch with you regularly. If something happens to the property, you must inform them no matter how late in the night it is.

- **Give them a welcoming gift:** If you want to make a lasting impression on your tenants, leave them a few nice gifts. This can include cleaning products, decor, things they can use in the kitchen, bathroom products, and others. Your tenants will be happy that you went the extra mile to get them some goodies.

- **Provide your tenant with two sets of keys:** If there is one sole tenant, then two sets of keys will be enough. This will ensure that the tenant will not have to worry about being locked out of their apartment or house. If there are storage units on the property, be sure to give them a set of keys to access it.

# Final Thoughts

Finally, you are able to rent out the property to a tenant. At this point, preparing the paperwork such as the contract or agreement will be one of your top priorities. Meanwhile, you might want to get started on advertising your vacancies.

When meeting with tenants, keep an eye out for any red flags. If you are good at picking up on things, you can make a decision in your mind to determine whether or not the person would make a great tenant or not. Once everything looks good, you can then give the tenant the lease agreement so they can sign, and they can move right in.

# Chapter 10: Business Is Business, Don't Think Otherwise

In this chapter, we're going to focus more on the administration end of your real estate business. We'll be talking about what you'll be doing in terms of your day-to-day tasks. This chapter will give you the ins and outs so you can build your business from the ground up.

You'll learn what an LLC is and what other business structures you can form in your business. We'll also discuss how you can put together your business advisory team. These are people who will help you set up your business and manage it wisely.

Speaking of managing, we'll discuss tips on how to manage your time wisely. And you'll learn how to become a business leader while becoming an effective investor at the same time. You'll learn how to develop systems while applying the relevant technology.

Lastly, we'll discuss what you'll need in your office. After all, you need a workspace to set up meetings with sellers, business partners, and those who are relevant to your success. Keep in mind that business is business, and it shouldn't be anything but that.

You're in the business of giving people a place to live while bringing in income to provide more property options for your tenants. So, it really shouldn't be considered a hobby of sorts. Let's get to it:

## LLC (Limited Liability Company) and Other Business Structures

Typically, you're going to consider setting up an LLC or a Limited Liability Company. This will give you sole proprietorship of the company. At the same time, it will give you liability protection and ensures that you won't be double taxed (unlike some business structures).

One of the best things about an LLC is that you are not liable for any business debts. On top of that, your business finances will be separate from your personal finances. Should anything happen in terms of legal issues, the business finances will be affected while your personal finances will not be subject to anything.

Depending on the state you live in, LLCs may have a limited lifespan. If a key figure of your business were to leave or join, you may need to dissolve or reform the LLC. For more information on how your LLC will work, take a look at your state's guidelines and laws.

## Other types of business structures

There are other options to structure your business aside from an LLC. Let's take a look at the following business structures and what their advantages and disadvantages are:

- **Sole proprietorship:** Aside from LLCs, this is one of the most common business structures. This is owned by one person. A sole proprietor will not produce a separate business entity. And therefore, business assets and liabilities are not separate from each other. Unlike an LLC, if your business goes into debt your personal finances may be affected as well.

- **Partnerships:** There are two kinds of partnerships: general and limited. A general partnership comprises two or more people while a limited partnership requires one general partner and one limited partner to start. While general partnerships are taxed at the personal income level, they have control and responsibility for the business. Meanwhile, a limited partner owns a portion of the company without taking any risks or responsibilities.

- **Corporation:** There are different types of corporations that you can form including a C Corp. In the eyes of the law, corporations are independent legal entities. Corporations are double taxes, meaning you pay income taxes twice. And they require a lot of recordkeeping and reporting in accordance with tax requirements and regulations. If you are new to the real estate business, refrain from forming a corporation as this might be complex.

- **S Corporation:** An S Corp is where profits and losses are passed through the personal income of the owner. Therefore, they are not subjected to a corporate tax. The owners and shareholders of an S Corp are taxed. If you want to incorporate without the double taxation, an S Corp may be a good decision.

## Create Your Business Advisory Team

Your business advisory team are the people you want to get in contact with each time you need assistance with a certain area of business. This includes the financial aspect of running a business and even those who are willing to help you understand the risks and complexities of real estate.

Who should be a part of your team? Here's a list of who you should include:

## 1. Accountant

No one knows numbers better than an accountant. In fact, they will give you the lowdown on how your company is performing financially. They will also help you decide whether or not the property you are interested in acquiring might be worth the investment.

They'll crunch your numbers, so you don't always have to. They will also help you prepare for purchasing a property and ensuring you have the budget to make the sale final. They will also handle the financial statements for the banks and handle any tax related business.

## 2. Banker

Having a banker as part of your advisory team is key. That's because they'll help you secure financing for any property acquisitions and even the expenses that go along with your real estate business. You may need something like a contingency fund for unexpected expenses, renovations for newly acquired properties, downtime for location changes, and more.

## 3. An attorney

Yes, real estate businesses will be dealing with the legality of things all the time. Everything from tenant contracts to taxes. This will be your legal advisor should there be any concerns regarding what you'll want to do in order to solve a problem (such as evicting a tenant). If you have any tax issues to contend with, a tax attorney knowledgeable with such laws will be of help.

## 4. Contractor

Most of the time, your properties will need a little fixing up. So, it would make sense to have a contractor that is known for doing plenty of renovations and repairs for residential properties. When looking for a contractor, be sure to get references from past clients before making a decision to bring them on.

### 5. Appraiser

An appraiser is someone you can contact whenever you want updated figures for a property's value. They can be very helpful especially if you plan on upping the rent in between tenants or selling the property outright. After they give you an estimation on the value, you can decide where to go from there.

### 6. Building inspector

This is someone who will inspect the property thoroughly so they can determine what may need to be fixed or replaced. This might be someone you have already worked with from the beginning when you first began to acquire properties. One reason why they are so important is because they see issues with the property that no one else does. They'll give you a good idea on how much you'll be spending on repairs.

## Managing Your Time

If there is one thing any business leader should do, it's manage their time wisely. We'll be taking a look at a few tips to help you maximize your time management, so you don't feel overwhelmed about the tasks at hand. Here are four things that you should do:

## 1. Always make notes

Sometimes, we forget things. Even the most important things. That's why you should write them down at the beginning and end of each day.

If it's something you really don't want to forget, write it down anyways. A relapse in memory happens. And it saves you a lot of time rather than wasting thinking about what it was.

Make sure that your list and notes are organized nice and neatly. That way, you can cross off one thing on the 'to-do' list before moving onto another.

## 2. Stick to the to-do list

When putting together a to-do list, you'll want to plan and prioritize everything. The tasks that require the most importance and urgency are done first. Following that, take a look at the tasks that are important, but not as urgent.

To give you a good understanding of how to organize and put together a task list, check out the 'Eisenhower Matrix'. It's a system that will allow you to separate tasks based on the importance and urgency. Remember, the tasks with the most importance and urgency are done first every single time.

## 3. Delegate any tasks if needed

There are larger tasks that need to be done. However, it might be too large for one person to do. That's where delegating comes into play.

You can delegate the small manageable tasks to those you employ. Meanwhile, you focus on the more important tasks that are related. For example, if you need to collect rent checks, you should consider collecting from tenants from letters A-N while another person collects checks from names O-Z.

Be sure to delegate any tasks so they are done quickly and efficiently each time.

## 4. Stay in contact with workers

As a business leader, you should always stay in contact with those you've employed. This is one more reason why maximizing and managing your time is important. You want tasks done quickly and efficiently.

Being in constant contact while also delegating any tasks to your workers will be the norm, you'll want to communicate with them on how the tasks must be done. Make sure the tasks are manageable for them and nothing is too complex. Don't be afraid to answer questions they may have.

## Looking for More Talent

Obviously, there's a lot of work that needs to be done in a business. So, your best solution would be hiring the right people. As long as you have the budget to hire talent, there is nothing stopping you bringing in a few extra hands.

When is it time to hire the right kind of people? Let's take a look at some scenarios:

### When you have several tenant applications

If and when you have several tenant applications to field through, it may seem like an overwhelming task for you. That's where hiring a property management company comes into play. Not only will they be knowledgeable in the application process, but they will be able to help process the applications and determine which applicants are considered qualified tenants based on the criteria set forth.

### Repairs are needed on a property

The damage may have been no fault of the tenant. Or maybe it was. Either way, hiring a contractor to fix the damage will be key.

However, this will depend on what needs to be fixed. Remember, contractors should be a part of your advisory team when you're running your real estate business.

## When administrative tasks are piling up

In any business, there are administrative tasks that will need to be fulfilled. And you can't do everything all at once. That's when you'll need to hire administrative assistants and the like.

They can do everything from booking appointments, connecting important people like clients and contractors to you, and everything in between.

## You're looking for new property to acquire

There will come a time when you want to add another piece of property to the portfolio. That's where you can hire someone who can scout out something that may be up for grabs. From there, that person will relay the information about the property such as the number of bedrooms and bathrooms, how much it's going for, and so on.

They can also assess whether or not the property may be worth acquiring based on walkability, its close proximity to points of interest, and so on.

## Evolving Your Skills and Becoming A Better Investor and Businessman

Being a business leader while being an effective investor at the same time will be vital in real estate. Not only will you be employing your most reliable employees, you'll also be looking out for more opportunities to further your business growth.

That's why it is always important to evolve your skills constantly so you can keep the business up and running for as long as you can. Here are some tips that will help you become better skilled at being an excellent business leader and investor:

### Build a competent staff

When it comes to hiring the right people, they need to be knowledgeable at what they do. If necessary, there may be people who will need to be trained. As such, they must be willing to learn and know what they are doing without making a lot of mistakes.

Hire people who should clearly understand their roles and responsibilities. Identify their strengths and consider them for positions that will help them put it to good use.

## Set SMART goals for your team

Setting Specific, Measurable, Attainable, Relevant, and Time-Bound goals are what makes business leaders great. As long as they are in alignment with the company's work and strategic plans, those goals can be accomplished.

## Reward your staff for a good performance

As an employer, it would be incumbent upon you to reward your staff for a good job performance. However, you must also know how to hold anyone accountable for doing less than their best.

## Know that each opportunity missed can be a blessing

You can't always win every investment opportunity there is. And you cannot be emotionally attached to them either. Sometimes, a missed opportunity is a blessing in disguise.

You will eventually find opportunities to grow your portfolio. And you also will need to accept the fact that the next opportunity may not come as quickly as the last one.

### Be ready to solve problems at any given time

A true business leader is someone who can solve a conflict at any time. He or she will look at the problem from different angles and find a creative solution. If there is tension between two employees, a leader can set each of them off to the side, listen to them, and come up with a solution based on what they hear.

The ability to resolve conflict in business will separate the true business leaders from those that may not be cut out for it.

## Developing Systems and Applying Technology

In business, you'll want to keep everything organized and working like a well-oiled machine. That's why you'll want to invest in software that may be beneficial for your real estate business. Take a look at some property management software that is available on the market.

For example, if you want something that will be great for DIY landlords, you can use Tenant Cloud. If you want something that is easily customizable, then Avail would be an excellent choice.

Also, you want to consider investing in software that will allow you to automate those small, mundane tasks. You can't spend the entire day doing small menial tasks when you have other priorities to focus on.

While you're at it, consider investing in a software that will allow tenants to interact with you and even send their rent payments online. Not only will it be easier for them to pay the rent, it will be easier for you to collect it without going door to door.

## Your Office, and Everything You'll Need in It

In today's business world, you have two choices for your office. You either rent a small space out or have a home office. If you don't want to spend a lot of money on office space, you can operate an office right out of your own home.

It would be nice to have an office since you'll be meeting with tenants, contractors, fellow investors, and those who you'll be interacting with on a regular basis. You don't need to go all out in order to impress clients and potential tenants.

At the same time, you'll want to use your office as a place where you can work and be free from distractions. This is your headquarters for your real estate business. But you won't need a lot of space if you have just a few people working for you.

### What you need for your office

When putting together your office, it's important to have the following things: a computer (linked to high-speed internet, a desk and a chair, paper shredder, printer, filing cabinet, and a fire-safe box. Just the basics will be enough to ensure that you operate like a business without all the bells and whistles.

## Final Thoughts

Your rental properties are all part of the business. You'll be making more than enough money to grow it even more if you so choose. When it comes to the formation, consider a business type that works best for you.

As a beginner, you may want to start off as an LLC since it provides you with a much easier structure compared to corporations. Remember to manage your time wisely and focus on priority tasks while automating the tasks that seem to be mundane and tedious.

You'll also want to delegate any tasks that you may not want to do to other employees. They may include taking calls and messages, scouting out properties, preparing the paperwork for tenants, contractors, others, and more. Don't forget to put together your business advisory team so you have a group of go-to people to consult with whenever you run into any problems.

# Chapter 11: Keeping the Properties in Perfect Condition and Interacting with Your Tenants

As a landlord, you will be saddled with responsibilities to ensure that your property is in good shape. At the same time, you also want to make sure that the tenants who occupy it are happy as well. In this chapter, we'll discuss what your roles, responsibilities, and rights are as a landlord.

While you are responsible for managing the property as you see fit, the tenant is responsible for following the lease agreement as outlined. One shared responsibility that both you and the tenant should have is communicating with each other on a regular basis.

That's because things like property damage can happen at any time. Or they may have some questions or concerns about the property itself. Either way, keeping the lines of communication open both ways will be essential.

Even your property managers (should you hire them), must also be willing to communicate with tenants on a regular basis. After all, the property must undergo routine inspections and maintenance (if needed). If the property is in good shape, the tenant is happy and so are you.

We'll also talk about how you can handle maintenance and repairs along with difficult or bad tenants. You'll also learn how to collect rent when the time comes. There are advantages and disadvantages to becoming a landlord, but we'll help you handle them in this chapter.

Also, we'll discuss specific tenant-centric situations such as when a tenant dies or if they outright abandon the property without warning. Lastly, we'll discuss what you need to do once a tenant moves out of your property.

If your goal is to keep your tenants happy, keep reading:

## Your Role, Responsibilities, and Rights as the Landlord

Let's take a look now at the roles, responsibilities, and the rights that you possess as a landlord:

## Warranty of Habitability

It is your responsibility to provide a place for a tenant that is habitable. This means that the conditions must be favorable for them to live in. This includes making sure that the structural integrity of the property is in good shape, keeping the HVAC, heating, water, and plumbing running properly, and complying with codes and regulations in accordance with local, state, and federal laws.

Also, you must fulfill any repair requests that are made by the tenant. You can do the repairs yourself or delegate the task to a handyman or contractor. Lastly, the property must be peaceful, quiet, free of hazards, and free of any invasive pests.

## A secure dwelling

Safety is paramount for a tenant. That's why you want to make sure that the locks on the property are in good working condition before a tenant moves in. No matter how safe a neighborhood can be, home invasions can happen anytime and anywhere.

You want your tenants to have peace of mind knowing that their locks are good to go (even when they are sleeping or away). Likewise, the landlord should also be responsible for ensuring a crime-free property by doing a criminal background check on every tenant application.

Making one wrong choice by moving in a tenant that may be a threat to the neighborhood should be the last thing you ever do. Especially if there's a chance they may re-offend again (depending on the crime). Assume that every property in the neighborhood is yours and make it your responsibility to keep the others safe.

## Making repairs

If you don't have any repair skills, you can always employ the services of a handyman or a contractor. If you have basic repair skills, then you can opt to use them. Things can and will break on the property (whether by fault or no fault of the tenant).

Tenants must put in a request for repairs if need be. The landlord must fulfill that request as soon as possible. This is one of the major reasons why the responsibility shared between the tenant and the landlord is communication.

However, if the damage is done by the tenant, you may be more inclined to defer the responsibility to the tenant to repair the damage. Which means the tenant will need to take care of the repair at their own expense (or the security deposit).

## Maintaining the property

The property must be maintained regularly. Which is why regular inspections are important. If and when an inspection is needed, it is important to make sure that you let the tenant know ahead of time (just so there are no surprises).

Meanwhile, you can also go out of your way to do small tasks to make the property look good. If there is a garden, tend to it when needed. If there is a need that appears to be fulfilled and the tenant doesn't notice, bring it up to them so they know what's going on.

## Collect rent

Every month (specifically on the first), rent is due. Which means you'll need to collect it from your tenants by rent check or any method of payment. If you have multiple tenants, this may be a difficult thing to do.

If you have multiple tenants, you may employ the responsibilities of a property management company to collect the rent on your behalf.

## The right to evict

As a landlord, you have the right to evict a tenant. It should be under the condition that the tenant broke the lease agreement in a grave violation. For example, a landlord can evict a tenant if the property is known for a place where illegal drugs are being sold.

If a lease agreement is broken by a tenant, it can result in an eviction. The question is: where will you draw the line? Typically, illegal activities that may draw constant police attention just might be the start.

## Communicating with Tenants

As stated earlier, you and the tenant have a shared responsibility. And that is to keep the lines of communication open between each other. The reason being is because things can and will happen anytime.

The both of you must communicate regularly and be transparent with one another. When the tenant first moves in, it's important to go over with them their rights and roles. What should they be reminded about?

Let's take a look at what the tenant is responsible for:

- **Keeping a line of communication open:** Enough said.

- **Report any damage or need for repairs promptly:** It doesn't matter if it's 5pm or 5am. If there is damage or a repair that is needed, it is the tenant's responsibility to give the landlord a heads up. That way, the issue is addressed quickly and thus the property is habitable once again. If the damage is caused by the tenant, it will be their responsibility to have it fixed at their own expense instead of yours.

- **Follow the lease agreement:** It's all there in writing. They have a responsibility to follow the agreement as it is seen fit. No illegal activity. Pay the rent on time. Maintain a healthy and safe environment. The list goes on and on. Just make sure that the tenant honors the agreement.

## Communication tips

- **Keep the door open:** To ensure that the lines of communication are open, have an open-door policy intact. This will benefit both you and the tenant. On top of that, it will place a high priority on tenants that want to be valued. Whether they have questions about the lease, rent extensions, or whatever it is, be willing to listen and have an answer.

- **Respond to repair requests ASAP:** We cannot stress this more, if the repair requests are made by a tenant, it is your responsibility to have them fulfilled quickly.

- **Have multiple lines of communication open:** It doesn't always have to be done by phone. Make sure that you and the tenant can communicate via text/SMS, email, or in-person. The more ways you and your tenant can communicate, the better.

- **Be honest and transparent:** Honesty and transparency goes a long way. And it's also a two-way street. This will lead to a healthy, long-term relationship with each other. Not only that, but a tenant will also need to be honest if they want a good rental reference from you.

- **Alert the tenants prior to any pre-planned activities:** These include repairs, regular maintenance, and showings. You'll want to let your tenants know ahead of time to ensure that the tenant's right to privacy is not violated.

## How To Handle Inherited Tenants

Inherited tenants are currently existing tenants from the previous property manager. This may happen down the road whenever you acquire additional properties. So already, you might have a new addition to your cash flow without doing a lot of work to fulfill vacancies (if any).

How do you handle inherited tenants, even though they might not know who you are? Let's take a look at the following tips:

### Note that you are handling someone else's issues

Truth be told, the issues the previous landlord is dealing with may also be yours. This includes dealing with tenants who may become a source of frustration for you. That is why it's important to gather all the information and intelligence you need (in a non-invasive way) on the tenants that reside on the property.

However, if you want to avoid any bad tenants or the like, it's important to consider taking this next tip to heart.

## Do your 'tenant diligence'

Just like due diligence, you want to know the kind of tenants you are dealing with before you buy the property. Looking before you leap comes in different ways. When you are touring the property, be sure to talk to as many tenants as possible.

They may already be aware that their current landlord may be selling the property. Plus, there may be no better time to establish the lines of communication with the people who could potentially become your tenants. From there, you can tell which ones will be good and which ones may be a cause for trouble.

## Let them know about any potential rule changes

With new landlords comes the idea of new changes in rules and policies. And for this reason, you're going to expect some pushback from tenants. It may almost end up getting to the point where the tenant may violate their lease and get evicted (which may not be the smart thing to do).

If there are any changes that you plan to make, be sure to go over it with your tenants so you can get some feedback from them. Implementing changes without warning will lead to angry tenants. In other words, don't make your first impression on them a bad one.

## Handling Maintenance and Repairs

One thing you need to ask yourself is should you handle the repairs and maintenance or not? The short answer: it depends. If you have one property and have basic repair skills, you can do it yourself.

However, if you lack the repair skills or if you have multiple properties, then you'll want to delegate those repair and maintenance responsibilities to the property management company. At the same time, you'll want to employ a handyman and have contractors on speed dial should any needs arise.

Keep in mind that if you plan on doing repairs and maintenance yourself, you may need the proper certification and the like in order to perform them. If this seems like you're going to jump through so many hoops, then it would be a better idea to defer all maintenance and repairs to those who already have the certifications and the like.

With that said, here are some other tips and considerations to keep in mind:

- **Always have a budget:** Repairs and maintenance will always come in a timely or untimely manner. Regardless, you'll need the money to pay for it. That is why your expenses for the month must include setting aside an amount of money to cover any incidental costs.

- **Let your tenants know ahead of time:** If and when repair requests are being made, it is your responsibility to let them know when the handyman or you will be arriving to make the repairs needed. This will give the tenant notice that the landlord will enter the property (regardless if they are at home or not). Also, this will give the tenant an opportunity to tidy up the place if needed.

- **Schedule inspections periodically:** You and the tenant must be aware that the property must be inspected to ensure things are in good shape. And that's where you need to let the tenant know ahead of time of when an inspection can take place. No need for surprises or anything of that nature.

## What to Do When Faced with Difficult or Bad Tenants

A difficult or bad tenant will be one of the biggest problems you'll run into. Not to mention, it's one of the most stressful. What will you do in an effort to deal with them accordingly?

Certainly, evicting them would be a solution. However, it has to be within a legal reason to do so. You cannot simply evict a tenant just because you can (considering the laws and regulations discouraging this).

What constitutes a difficult or bad tenant? This could be someone who may be committing illegal activities on the property such as selling drugs. Or this could be someone who could be making a lot of noise to draw the ire of their neighbors.

Even if you are dealing with a difficult tenant, you must take the following into consideration in a professional manner:

### Lay down clear rules

It's your property and it's your rules. Those rules must be honored by the tenant. At the same time, those rules must be outlined in the lease agreement.

If the lease agreement is violated, that can give you the opportunity to evict the tenant if it is warranted. You want the tenant to make sure they understand and be aware of these rules. This way, they won't use the 'I misunderstood the rules' excuse.

## Use any line of communication possible, including digital

Whether it's by phone, text, or social media, you want to communicate with the tenant as best as you can. Whether they respond to you or not will be in their court. Also, make sure that the lines of communication stay open no matter what. One last thing, keep a record of every bit of communication between you and the tenant. This way, should any legal issues arise, you can use this in your case if it ever goes to court.

## Be patient

Yes, we know that difficult tenants can be a pain in the...well, you know. But no matter what, you'll want to be patient with them. Again, the way you handle the situation may be brought up in a court of law should things go into a legal battle.

## Set deadlines

Rents are due the first of the month. The leases expire at the end of a specific month after a period of time (i.e. -- 12 months). Simple as that.

And you want the tenants to respect and meet those deadlines in a timely manner. If for some reason the tenant may have missed a deadline, give them breathing room such as a grace period.

## Begin the eviction process if all else fails

If you have exhausted every possible option there is. And the tenant seems to give you grief. At this point, you know what to do.

If the tenant has repeatedly broken the lease agreement, it will be in your legal rights to evict them off your property. If they miss rent payments, refuse to move out after the lease expires, or violated the terms, those are grounds for eviction.

Law enforcement may need to get involved if needed. Especially if the tenant is doing something illegal on the property (and on a regular basis).

## Preventative measures

Screening tenant applications and checking for references is always the best line of defense in keeping bad tenants out. That's why you want to go as deep as possible when looking through every application. When you hear of anything about a difficult tenant and you notice a pattern through other references, that's a no brainer to deny the applicant.

## Why a tenant must move out, if needed

- **Missed rent payments:** Simply put, if a tenant cannot pay their rent on time constantly and always delays them, you know it will hurt you financially. If they frequently miss payments and grace periods, that's when you need to evict them as soon as possible.

- **Illegal activities:** Safety is your number one priority. And you want to be considerate of the neighbors that live nearby. Once again, assume that every neighboring property is yours. And you are responsible for the safety and security of the inhabitants. Law enforcement may need to be involved if push comes to shove.

- **Lease expiration:** The tenant has the responsibility to renew the lease or allow it to expire. In the event of the latter, they must be prepared to move out the day of the lease expiration. Otherwise, if they occupy the property beyond that, it may be an issue that you need to work out. If they refuse to leave, you must get law enforcement involved since the tenant is technically trespassing.

## Everything You Need to Know About Collecting Rent

Collecting rent may seem like a simple task to do as a landlord. However, it's not as easy as you think. That's because not every tenant that resides on your properties will pay on time, every time.

This section will show you everything you need to know about collecting rent including the best practices. You'll also learn what to do if a tenant does not pay rent or you receive a bounced check. We'll also discuss grace periods and extensions.

### Tips on collecting rent on time, every time

**Set up online payments:** In today's digital world, automation is king. Especially when it comes to collecting rent. The best way to collect rent is by working with the tenant to where it can be set up digitally. This way, the rent will be paid for by the tenant every first of the month. There is plenty of software and apps that you and the tenant can use to take care of this.

**Collect in person:** Collecting in person is never out of the question. Especially if you or the tenant are not so technologically inclined. However, if you have more than one property, this process will be difficult. You don't want to be driving from one location to another and then another all day long. Not only that, but you also don't know if the tenant is going to be around when you're there. Alternatively, a property manager can collect the rent on your behalf.

**Drop box:** Because of the likelihood of in-person payments not being done regularly, a drop box might be the next best solution. This will work to your advantage if the property is a multi-family home. This can also work if you have a few properties of your own. If you do have a drop box, make sure it has the proper security like a security camera so you can deter and prevent theft from occurring.

**Checks by mail:** If you really want to go old school, consider accepting the checks by mail. If you are uncomfortable giving tenants your home address, then set up a post office box and have the tenants send you the checks that way.

## What happens if a tenant misses a rent payment?

Missed rent payments will happen. And if that does, it would be up to you on how to handle it.

One way to do this is provide a grace period for the tenant. This allows the tenant to pay the rent within that period without a late fee. For example, you can allow a grace period for 15 days.

After that, if the tenant pays the rent, they may be subject to a late fee. If you issue an eviction notice after that grace period, remind them that the notice will be null and void if the payment is made (plus a late fee).

One thing to keep in mind is that a missed payment may be due to circumstances on the tenant's end. They may have lost a job, got robbed, or something may have occurred beyond their control. This is one good reason why both tenants and landlords should communicate regularly with each other.

## What if a rent check bounces?

One such situation that can take place is a rent check being bounced. And this can hurt your bank account in a few days. That is why it is important to implement a policy in the lease that will ensure that the tenant 'shall pay' a fee should the rent check be returned due to insufficient funds.

Depending on your state, you may also sue the tenant to reimburse any losses if a rent check bounces.

## When a Tenant Dies

If a tenant dies whether on the rental property or elsewhere, you have your rights to handle such a situation. However, there is a certain protocol that you must follow. Here are the steps that need to be taken should a tenant pass away:

### 1. Get a written notification

This written notification should be procured by the tenant's next of kin or the executor of their estate. Either way, the landlord will find out about it. This notification shall be required in order to begin the termination of the lease via the legal channels.

## 2. Secure the property as soon as possible

From there, you'll want to secure the property as soon as possible. This will prevent unauthorized individuals from entering the property and attempting to remove the deceased tenant's possessions. At the same time, you'll want to consider using the emergency contact or next of kin as the designated person to receive any possessions that will be removed from the property.

If the tenant has died on the property and you were notified, be sure to notify the authorities and the emergency contact. Be sure to follow any local or state laws that are applicable to securing the property or the possessions of the deceased tenant.

## 3. Return the security deposit

After the property has been vacated and the deceased tenant's possessions have been removed, do a check of the property. Check for any damage, wear, tear, or the like. Once complete, you can return the tenant's security deposit (or a portion of it) to the next of kin or the executor of the estate.

### 4. Go through the legal channels to terminate the lease

Just because a tenant dies, doesn't mean the lease is terminated automatically. This will also depend on the type of lease. If it's a month-to-month lease, the death will serve as a thirty (30) day notice and thus allow the lease to expire as is. However, if it is a long-term lease, then the landlord can allow the lease to end early.

In the event of the latter, please contact your attorney to see what can be done so there is no burden placed upon you or the deceased tenant's family. From there, you can also prepare the property for the next tenant.

## Dealing with Abandonment

There will be tenants who will up and leave the property for no apparent reason. They'll just outright abandon it and never return. In the event that this does happen, it's important to take the right action.

At this point, you'll have to perform a protocol that can last as much as 8 weeks. First, you'll want to serve a first warning notice to a tenant. You will request that they pay rent within an eight-week period.

If there is no response after a couple of weeks, issue a second warning. If the tenant does not respond after the second, issue a third and final warning on a much noticeable area of the property. The third warning must be issued at least 5 days before the 8-week period set in the first notice has expired.

If the tenant does respond to the notices, the procedure will end. However, if the tenant does not return, you are within your legal right to enter the property under the one of the following conditions:

- The property is in a condition that is considered insecure
- If there are any damages or dangers to the property (including electrical and gas appliances)

During the abandonment process, you'll want to get in contact with the tenant's emergency contact in an attempt to locate them. At the same time, check to see if they are actually still paying rent. Lastly, check the utilities to ensure that they are in good working order.

If the property is indeed abandoned, you'll want to consult with any local and state laws that allow you to enter the property and remove any possessions that belong to the tenant. Make sure that they are stored properly and send a notice of storage to the tenant or the emergency contact.

## What to Do After A Tenant Moves Out

When a tenant moves out, usually they'll do it with prior notice. At that time, you can advertise the vacancy immediately. This will ensure that it can be fulfilled as soon as possible (and when the old tenant moves out).

On the day of the move out, you and the tenant should go over the property one last time. Check for any damages, malfunctions, or the like. After the inspection is complete, you can hand over the security deposit (either in full or partially if there is any damage or wear).

The tenant must hand over the keys to you on the day they move out. After the tenant has left, be sure to change the locks before the new tenant moves in. And for good measure, inspect the property once more to see if everything is in good condition and working properly.

## Final Thoughts

Your tenants will be good to your properties if you choose the right ones. Keep in mind that each of you have roles and responsibilities. And you both need to do your part to ensure that the property is in good condition.

Both you and the tenant must communicate regularly. Also, you'll want to notify the tenant ahead of time if you plan on being on the property for inspections or maintenance. When dealing with bad or difficult tenants, you'll want to ensure that they have broken the lease agreement in some way prior to evicting them.

If a tenant dies or has abandoned the property, you'll want to follow the specific procedures outlined for such events. Either way, this may also require you to consult your attorney to ensure that you follow any legal protocols and procedures. When a tenant is about to move out, your job is to make sure that the vacancy is fulfilled as soon as possible.

That way, when the old tenant moves out, you can prepare the property for the new one. And the whole cycle starts all over.

# Chapter 12: Establish Your Real Estate Network Even If You Are Investing in Rental Properties

As someone who invests in rental properties, you are technically involved in the world of real estate. So, it wouldn't hurt for you to establish your network. Imagine having a robust network of real estate professionals that you can work with in various situations.

You may know someone who is looking to purchase a house. They may be looking for a certain property and you might just know the person that sells it. Aside from that, this is a network of people you can provide value for.

We'll talk about how you can build your network in the real estate world and where you can find them. We'll also discuss the importance of real estate clubs, what they are, and why joining one is a must. By the end of the chapter, you'll also learn how to build a database of not just real estate professionals, but also tenants, agencies that will connect tenants to property managers, and more.

When it comes to building networks, you'll want to make sure that your ability to communicate and build relationships is on point. You'll learn the ins and outs of those in this chapter. Ready to build your real estate network for the better?

Let's get crackin':

## Networking in The World of Real Estate

If you want to be successful in real estate, then it's best to build a network that will help you out. Especially if you are looking to connect with real estate professionals and others who may be associated with them. The first thing you need to ask is where you should begin.

Let's take a look at a few places where you can start building your network:

### Online databases

Today, almost every real estate professional in the world has some kind of online presence. To begin, you can take a look at online databases. You can whittle down the location, the type of real estate business they do, and so on.

From there, you can get their contact information and send them a message. Even though you are someone who invests in rental properties, you at least know enough of the language that the real estate professionals speak. But don't say a lot of it just to impress them or bend over backwards.

## Social media

Yes, social media is a great place to connect with real estate professionals. Most of them may be found via LinkedIn or Facebook. You may also connect with real estate professionals in dedicated social media groups.

You can find groups that are focused on local real estate professionals and even those in a much larger region. Either way, join as many of these social media groups as possible.

## Networking events

If there are any networking or industry events in the area, you'd be insane not to go to them. This will give you a good opportunity to meet with local and regional real estate professionals face to face. This will also give them a chance to get to know you in a different way as opposed to exchanging phone calls and emails.

## Real Estate Investing Clubs

A real estate investing club might be something that you're interested in joining. You can join one yourself so long as you have your own money to invest in. People who are retired, students, wealthy business owners, and everyone in between can join these clubs.

Typically, a real estate investor club is small in size. Usually, you'll have five to ten people in a single club. All of which have the same investment goals even though there are not legal limits or minimums to deal with. Members of these clubs pool their money together and will make investment decisions as a group.

You can see if you can join an existing club if there is one in your area. However, if you so desire, you can create one. This is one of the reasons why you should always be building a real estate network, even if you invest in rental properties.

In fact, you could get other real estate investors in your network to join you. And from there, once it's established, you and the rest of the club can begin to make investment decisions using the money that you all have pooled together.

## Creating Your Database

If you're going to build a network, you're going to have to put together a database. This way, you'll know who is who and you'll be able to connect with them so long as you have the right contact information. On top of that, you'll have a list of people that you can use to connect one person to the other that is in your network.

For example, if you have an old tenant that wants to rent a property from another landlord, you can make the connection from there. This will make it easy on the tenant because you serve as a rental reference that can put in a good word for them.

Your databases should be kept separate, first and foremost. Second, your databases should be assigned with the following labels:

- **Buyers**
- **Sellers**
- **Tenants (past and present)**
- **Real Estate Agents or agencies**
- **Brokers**
- **Contractors**
- **Bankers and financial professionals**
- **Attorneys**

Whenever someone in your network (or outside of it) may need something, you'll know exactly who to connect them to. You can give that person value just by leveraging your real estate network. Even if it's a tenant that does not plan on renting from you, you can always refer them to other landlords as a gesture of goodwill.

Also, having a database of buyers will also serve as an excellent backup plan for rental properties. Because you might have someone who might be willing to rent a place if things fall through with a previous tenant. Or, if you are ready to sell a rental property, you can find a good buyer who will be willing to pay a good price for it.

Any way you slice it, there's always more than one way to leverage your network. And having neat, nicely organized databases with their own labels will be just the start. Use them to your advantage and you will be known as that person who is the ultimate connector.

Imagine being the go-to person and having them access your network of people. There could be property investors looking to get in the business and wanting to connect with you as well. So, things seem to come full circle because at one point, that new property investor was you.

# Establishing Your Presence and Building Relationships

If you're planning on building your network, it's better to establish a presence both online and/or offline. Without it, no one will know that you exist. In today's technology driven world, an online presence is a must.

But that doesn't mean you shouldn't leave out the idea of building an offline presence. Let's take a look now at the ways you can build an online presence:

## 4 Ways to Build Your Online Presence

### Start a website

To start, you should consider building a website if you want to establish a good online presence. That way, when people search for landlords or real estate professionals in their local area, they'll be able to know that someone exists.

You can also include things like a blog and even a listing of your currently vacant properties. As for the blog aspect of the site, don't talk about your personal life or anything like that. Instead, use the blog to provide some kind of value.

For example, you can write blog posts that are targeted towards tenants who may be looking for a place to rent but don't know how to fill out the application properly. Another post would be dedicated towards how they can automate their rental payments. Using the blog to provide some kind of value to tenants and real estate professionals alike will help you stand out more.

### Social media

Social media seems to be building up by the day. And as a real estate investor, you can even use it to show off your properties that are available. Your potential tenants may be looking for a place and are using every channel imaginable to find something.

You could set up a Facebook page and post pictures of a vacant property so prospective tenants know what they are looking at. The posts should be straightforward, to the point, and contain clear, easy to look at photos of the property.

You can also use social media as a way to get in contact with potential tenants should they have questions about the property, the application process, and so on.

### Paid advertising

There will come a time where vacancies need to be fulfilled. And you'll want to advertise your properties both online and offline. You can use paid advertising such as Facebook or Google ads.

The cool thing about paid advertising is that it will help get more eyeballs on the property and even some click throughs. You may even get online applicants using this method. Especially if all the potential tenant has to do is apply online (or even in person).

### Local directories and databases

If you really want to put yourself out there, don't stop with a website or social media. You can sign up for local directories and databases. Some of them may require a fee to be on the list for a period of time (while others like online databases may not).

## Building an offline presence

### Flyers

As mentioned before, flyers are a great way to put yourself out there. One of the best times to do this is whenever you have a property that has a vacancy that is waiting to be fulfilled. Remember to post these in high-traffic areas in your locale.

### Classified/Newspaper Ads

Classified and newspaper ads will usually give you a space for cheap. You can pay for a small space or pay even more for something larger.

## Communication Is Key

Networking requires one thing: communication. And nothing but communication. That's because you are talking with fellow investors, real estate professionals, tenants, and everyone that is involved in the process in some way.

It takes strong communication skills to succeed in the real estate business. And the same can be said about building your network. Let's take a look at some of the following tips that you'll need in order to make communication worth it in building your network:

1. Stay friendly and professional

Needless to say, effective communication in networking must always be friendly and professional. You want to sound like someone you can trust (while being that person that can be trusted by someone). Also, it's good to maintain a positive mental attitude while communicating with others.

2. Emphasize with people and their needs

If there is one thing that you absolutely need in terms of being an excellent communicator, it's having empathy. A client may have concerns about acquiring a property. A potential tenant may have concerns about the area that they are living in.

The list goes on and on. And it's important for you to understand their concerns while listening to exactly what they are dealing with. Plus, when you listen, you'll be able to come up with ideas and solutions on the fly.

The same goes when people are having frustrations that people are facing in the market. Don't be afraid to ask questions about the issue that's facing them. For example, ask someone who may be buying a house about what they are looking for in an agent.

If you are talking to tenants, ask them what they are looking for in an ideal rental situation? There are questions that are tailor made to any person you talk to when it comes to real estate.

## 3. Always follow-up or call back

The ability to follow up or call-back goes both ways. Don't be the person that calls once, talks to someone, and is never heard from again after that. Not only will that leave a bad impression, but that won't fare well with others who want to communicate with you.

If you are promising to call someone back, do good on that promise.

## 4. Ask questions

Seems simple enough, right? Ask questions that may address any issues a client may have. Ask questions to an attorney about a certain process that works with leases.

When talking with buyers or sellers, ask relevant questions such as 'what are they looking for in an agent?'. If it's someone selling a house, ask them what is motivating them to sell.

The deeper you dig, the more you'll learn to understand others who may be in the same situation in the future.

## Final Thoughts

Even if you invest in rental properties, you are still part of the real estate ecosystem. This means you can still build your real estate network from the ground up. And make sure you have one that is well-built so you can connect one person to the other if needed.

Be sure to meet with real estate professionals and everyone else who may also be involved with the process. Establishing long-term relationships with people in your network will pay off in the long run. Who knows...someone may also look to you for advice on real estate investing as well.

Remember, if you want to build a strong real estate network, having strong communication is your number one asset. Without it, you'll more than likely be going nowhere. Another thing to place a lot of importance on is your presence both online and offline.

People need to know that you exist. That way, they can contact you with questions, concerns, or if they just want to rent a property from you. The ability to communicate and be visible is just a couple of keys to success in real estate.

# Chapter 13: Marketing Your Way on Rental Properties

Without marketing, nothing would ever be sold. Or even rented for that matter. That's why the best thing to do when you need to fulfill a vacancy on your rental property is to get the word out.

This chapter will be dedicated to just that. We'll be talking about the real estate market in general. From there, we'll also talk about your marketing plan and how to execute it. In today's world, a lot of real estate investors will likely go the digital route.

However, you're going to learn how to implement some nice 1-2 punches using a combination of digital marketing and traditional marketing. Plus, we'll give you some marketing tools that you can use to your advantage.

Simply put, the first thing that you need to realize is an effective marketing campaign needs to start by knowing where the 'starving crowd' is. Where do they hang out? What exactly are they looking for?

You cannot simply just spread-out flyers and digital ads without knowing some insights and information about the market itself. Let's get right into the action so you have a marketing plan that you can put together and hit the ground running with it:

## The Real Estate Market

First, we'll be taking a look at the real estate market. It's true that it consists of buyers and sellers. However, what kind of market is it?

It could be a seller's market or a buyer's market. The best way to tell which is which is based on the conversations you hear. Another way of finding out is evaluating the market.

You can evaluate the market based on these two steps: analysis of the city and the neighborhoods within the cities of interest. How do you make an accurate analysis of both? Let's start with the city analysis:

### City analysis

To get a good idea of whether or not a city has a robust real estate market, we'll have to look at the following:

- **Job market:** If the job market is on the upswing, chances are there's a growing demand for housing. This is a good sign, especially for those investing in rental properties. There are major cities that serve as major hubs for several industries. Even the suburbs of these major cities would be ripe for rental properties.

- **Tourism:** Some cities will have a thriving tourism industry, and some may not. In a tourist centric city, this is a hotbed for Airbnb properties. That's because people will eschew the traditional find a hotel idea and find a place to crash like a spare bedroom or an apartment.

- **The price to rent ratio:** If you want a true market analysis number to work with, the price to rent ratio will be your best friend here. This will help you determine the demand for rental properties in the area. The higher the ratio, the more renters there are than homeowners.

- **Property taxes:** Property taxes are one of the most common expenses that investors face. However, the lower they are, the better. Keep in mind that larger cities will command higher property taxes compared to properties in the suburbs.

## Neighborhood analysis

While analyzing the neighborhoods of a city, you'll want to see what's close by (i.e. -- a one mile radius) and take notes. How far are the available rental properties from a grocery store or a school? Is it closer to a medical facility?

Typically, you'll want to find a rental property that is close by to some amenities that are easily accessible. To take it a step further, get a list of major employers for the area. What's the average commute time for residents in that neighborhood?

If you want to go a little deeper, there are heat maps that you can find on various real estate websites. These heatmaps will help determine which areas are valuable and which are not based on factors like walkability, commute time, and so on.

You can also whittle it all down using data such as listing price, average rental income, cash-on-cash-return, and more.

## Your Marketing Plan

This is where you want to put together a killer marketing plan. As mentioned before, the first rule of marketing is knowing where the fish are. In other

words, you need to know where you can find the 'starving fish'.
Even if you know where the starving fish are, you still need to get the offer and the message right. Otherwise, it will fall flat. With that said, we'll be sharing with you the following tips that will help you put together and execute a marketing plan that can work to your advantage.

Let's take a look at what you need to do:

## 1. What is your marketing philosophy?

Your marketing philosophy should be simple. You're looking at this as an investment rather than an expense. This should be your marketing philosophy to begin with.

At some point, you know that you're going to generate leads and potentially applicants that may become tenants. Now, let's discuss your goals and objectives.

## 2. What are your goals and objectives?

This is where you want to sit down with your business advisory team and discuss what kind of goals you want to set for your marketing strategy. This includes evaluating the levels of growth and your current position in the market space.

Next, you'll want to make a list of marketing goals. Then choose the top three to five goals that you feel are most important and go from there. Be sure to choose the goals that are actually measurable and hold yourself accountable towards them.

## 3. Setting your strategies

This is a step that you do not want to skip. Because strategy is a lot better than just tactics. As the old saying goes, tactics without strategy is like a car without a steering wheel.

Your strategies could be increasing awareness for your brand, generating leads, or increasing your sales overall. Since you're going to be fulfilling vacancies, you want to focus on lead generation since you want to generate interested applicants.

## 4. What are the tactics you want to use?

Make sure that your strategy and tactics do go together. Tactics are specific actions that you need to take in order to achieve your goals. For example, if your strategy is generating leads, what kind of actions are you going to take?

Are you going to take a digital approach and see what sticks? Or are you going to start out with a more traditional marketing approach? Or why not both?

If you want to generate awareness about how a tenant can be approved for an application, you can write a blog post on your website about the pertinent information they'll need to add when applying. The strategy is generating awareness and the tactic is posting something on your site that will get someone to take action.

See where we're going with this? With the right strategy comes the right tactics that will make it work.

## 5. What is your budget?

Your marketing budget must be enough to where you're able to fulfill the goals and objectives of your company. At the same time, you want to determine how soon you want to fulfill these vacancies. Aside from money, your time and resources will play a role in marketing your rental properties.

Before the marketing plan is executed, consider the amount of time and manpower it will take. Evaluate this with your team regularly to determine its progress and whether or not adjustments have to be made, if necessary.

## Traditional Marketing

The good news about traditional marketing: it has not gone the way of the dinosaur due to the Internet. The even better news: there's less competition that you'll have to deal with. And it is still as effective today as it was before the Internet had ever been introduced to the world.

What exactly are the traditional ways of marketing your rental properties? Let's take a look at them:

- **Classified ads:** You find them in newspapers and local guides where people are looking to sell things. The more money you spend, the greater the space. Plus, you can advertise in local or large regional periodicals and newspapers.

- **Flyers:** You probably see them every day at supermarkets, banks, drug stores, and so on. One of the reasons why flyers stand out is because you can give people a preview of what the property looks like.

- **Business cards:** You can leave business cards on bulletin boards or leave them at local businesses where your ideal market hangs out. Or you can talk to the manager of a business and ask about leaving a stack of business cards and hand them out whenever someone mentions about finding a place.

- **Signs/billboards:** If you have a property already acquired, you can use signs or billboards indicating that a place is for rent. From there, the call to action is simple: apply now.

- **Direct mail:** Indeed, direct mail still works. You can send it to a list of people who are looking to sell their homes and want to spend less money on living expenses. Or you can do a direct mail campaign with the goal of generating awareness. You buy the home they're selling and explain what your plans are with it.

- **Word of mouth/referrals:** This is one of the best reasons why you should always be building your network. Someone may be looking for a place. And someone within your network may serve as the bridge for that person to connect with you. Never count out word of mouth or referrals as a way to fulfill your vacancies.

## Digital Marketing

Digital marketing is targeted, and laser focused. It's not as broad reaching as traditional means. However, the issue here is that the competition can be fierce. But mixing some traditional with digital never killed anyone.

Let's take a look at some digital strategies that you can employ:

- **PPC ads:** These include Facebook ads, Google ads, or even banner ads. PPC ads charge per click. You can set it to where a specific demographic, local area, gender, and so on can see it while the rest that are outside of the target market cannot.

- **Social media:** Simply put, social media is being used a lot. And you can use your fan page or business page to post listings to your followers. The goal here: get your followers to share your vacancies with those who may be interested in finding a place.

- **Website:** A website may be a great place to do some digital marketing. Specifically, if you are using blog content to provide value to potential renters or even home sellers. This will also help establish your online presence and let people know that you are the real deal.

## Marketing Tools

There are plenty of real estate marketing tools out there (both free and paid). What can you use based on your budget and your goals? It's important to explore your options so you know which ones will work for you.

Let's take a look at some of the tools you can use:

### Facebook/Google Ads

This is a paid tool depending on the budget you set. You can set your ad budget to $5 per day if you want to and it can still generate leads. However, the higher the budget, the more people you'll reach.

## Real estate listings (MLS)

You can advertise your vacancies on real estate listings or even multiple listing services (MLS). Your properties can be listed on Zillow or Apartments.com (and similar sites). Use these listing sites to optimize your listing data and also get reviews that will be useful to you whenever you have more vacancies available.

## Social media

Social media is free to use (unless you are using their ad platforms). Yet, you can market your properties at any time. Or for a small amount of money, you can 'boost' your post so you can get more eyeballs without having to rely on the ad platforms.

## Email marketing

Your website will have an opt-in box that will allow people the opportunity to stay in the know about local properties that are up for rent. But having them give you their email address won't be easy. So, offer something in exchange such as a free guide for potential renters or house sellers. Something that will be valuable for them. From there, you can send regular newsletters and emails about property vacancies and other information that is relevant and valuable to your target market.

### Postcards

We're not just talking about those postcards you send on vacation. These are small postcards that you can buy for cheap. A stack of 100 will be $10 or less (depending on where you get them). Using a mailing list of home sellers, you send them a personalized postcard indicating your interest in the property. In fact, direct mail is most effective because no one ever spams a physical mailbox (other than bill collectors).

## Final Thoughts

Your marketing strategy will require a starving market, the right message, and possibly the right 'offer' (in this case, your rental properties). Your marketing message should target the right people while being able to 'exclude' those who may not fit the profile of your ideal tenant.

To make it effective, consider doing a mix of both traditional and digital marketing. However, you want to consider how much your budget will allow. Before you execute your marketing strategy, know what your goals are.

Once you have a goal in mind, find the right strategy and tactics that will help you reach them. It may take time, resources, and money. But when done right, you can generate leads and get the right tenants to rent from you.

# Chapter 14: Building A Long-Term Wealth and Passive Income with Rental Properties

One of the reasons why many people become real estate investors is to make money. And that's one of your goals (assuming you have picked up this book). It is possible to build long-term wealth and even passive income with rental properties.

However, as we've said before in the beginning, this is not a get rich quick scheme. This will take time to get you to your financial goals. At this point, we're pretty sure that you understand this.

In this chapter, we'll be talking about the basics of handling your finances. Also, we'll explain why achieving long-term wealth and passive income is possible with rental properties. But the thing is, once you have it going to where it generates passive income, it doesn't stop there.

We'll talk about what else you need to do now that you have the income you want. Also, you'll learn how to generate more income while keeping expenses low. Lastly, you'll learn that managing real estate taxes is still something that you need to keep an eye on (especially when there always is a potential for change).

Now, let's talk about the financials:

## Learn the Basics of Handling Finance, and Develop It from There

Basic finances may seem simple to do. You take the income, minus the expenses, and you get a profit or a loss. With real estate, the concept is the same but it's a little different. Here's what you need to know about basic finances involving real estate:

### Keeping personal and business finances separate

This must be rule number one in business finance. Keep your business bank account separate from your personal account. This means that all your business income and expenses must be subtracted from your business bank account.

Also, keep all receipts and paperwork in a separate file folder that indicates all things business. The same must go for your personal finances. Doing this properly will not only make things easier on you, but when tax time comes, you'll also get some sweet deductions for your business.

## Open separate accounts for your rental properties

To ensure that everything is kept separate, make sure that you open separate bank accounts. Specifically, you want to open one up for each rental property. This will keep the income and expenses separate from the other properties (and keep things well organized).

You'll get profit and loss statements, easily reconcile your bank account, and be able to file taxes easily without doing a lot of number crunching. You'll easily identify which bank account is tied to your rental property by organizing them by file folder, account number, and so on.

## Always track expenses

It cannot be stressed enough. Track every single dang expense that goes towards your rental properties. It will help you out during tax season. And it will give you an accurate account of everything.

Since you must keep financial records of every rental property in a separate folder, be sure to make a note of which expense is tied to whatever property that it went towards. For example, write down the address of the property so you can positively identify it.

Also, remember what your expenses are in terms of your rental properties. These include your marketing and advertising, property management fees, repairs and maintenance, and more. These are known as your operating expenses.

## Automate some tasks

There are some tasks that are so tedious and simple to do, they can be automated. When doing this with numerous rental properties, it can get to a point where it can consume your entire day. For this reason, you can automate the tasks, so you don't have to do the same thing all day long.

If there's a small task, automate it. This will free up a lot of time so you can focus on other business priorities.

## Prepare ahead of time

In business, a lot of people are forecasting their income and expenses. This is why it's important to always check on lease agreements and when they are due to expire. Also, you want to make forecasts that are based on certain situations (such as whether a tenant renews a lease or not).

Either way, prepare ahead of time for any changes in income and expenses (whether a tenant moves out or new tenants are moved into a property you recently acquired).

## Know your tax forms

The tax forms that you need to familiarize yourself with are W-9 and 1099 forms (among others). A W-9 form is a contractor's tax form that determines the type of business that you are. A 1099 form will be used for those who are self-employed (and make over $600 or more from their business).

These are basic tax forms that you'll want to use when the time comes to file them. If you have any questions or need to know any additional tax information, then talk to a tax expert or a CPA.

## Hire a CPA

A CPA is someone you should already have in your network (and your business advisory group). These people crunch numbers like no one's business. And they will give you advice on how to handle your finances.

They'll also analyze your financial performance based on the properties you own and the business finances as a whole. They will also help you during tax season when the time comes to pay them.

## Achieving Long-Term Wealth Is Definitely Possible

It's possible to achieve long-term wealth. But as we've said before, it takes time to get there. At the same time, it also takes properly managing your finances, the property itself, and everything in between to get there.

The key is doing it properly. You need to make sure that the income and expenses are calculated accurately. Second, you want to keep your tenants happy. And third, you need to be smart with the properties you want to invest in.

It will take one wrong move to further delay your progress (or blow it all up entirely). Here are some tips to achieve long-term wealth with rental properties:

### Make sure to pay off everything on-time, every time

You can pay off loans and that will take care of one expense that you'll no longer pay for. Once your debt is paid off, you don't have to worry about losing a ton of money.

## Always start out small

We all start somewhere. It might as well be from the ground level. With real estate, starting out can be as small as a single-family property.

From there, you can build your way up and acquire another property and repeat the process as many times as needed. The more properties you acquire, the more income you'll have. Sounds simple enough, right?

However, this is something that will take time. So, don't rush into buying another property when you know that you're going to need a little extra cash first and foremost. Your next property acquisition may be even more challenging than the last (so will things like repairs and the like).

## Hold, don't sell

Simply put, the best way to generate long-term wealth with rental properties is holding onto your rental properties. Don't sell them at all. Even if the properties don't have a mortgage anymore since you paid them off, you can enjoy getting a little extra money in your pocket.

It's as simple as that. When you see that bump in income after paying off some expenses, you'll be feeling pretty good.

## Turning It to Passive Income

Passive income is a lot of fun to have. Especially when you're earning a lot of money per month from your rental properties. And it's actually fairly easy to do once you know how to do it properly.

What you do with your passive income is entirely up to you. You can build a retirement fund, go on vacation, achieve financial freedom, and so on. The sky is pretty much the limit.

With that said, here are some tips to keep in mind while you are looking to generate passive income:

**Have enough cash flow:** Pretty much self-explanatory. If you have enough cash flow, you'll be able to generate passive income for each property. But remember, the market can change course over time. And because of that, the numbers can and will change.

**Screen your tenants properly:** Whether it's you or the property managers you hire, you want to make sure you screen and choose the right tenants. These are people who are reliable, willing to stay on for the long-term, and won't cause any trouble. A bad tenant is actually worse than no tenant at all, so screen wisely.

**Collect rent promptly:** The lease agreement should be clear enough to both you and the tenant. The rent must be collected on time and every time. Even though you might be the most laid back and chill person on the planet, you have to draw the line somewhere in terms of collecting rent. This way, it doesn't give tenants the opportunity to take advantage of you and skip out on rental payments.

## What's Left for You to Do?

Just because you have money rolling into your bank account, doesn't mean that's it. It doesn't mean sit back and relax. There are some things that you need to do while you are generating income from your rental properties.

Here are some things that you should do:

**Check the properties regularly:** Communication is important. So always check on the properties on a regular basis. Talk to the property managers and the tenants. Check to see if everything is fine. If there is a problem, address it promptly.

**Avoid legal trouble:** Legal issues can arise at any given time. That's why it is important to check the properties regularly and listen to your tenants if something is wrong. Also, be mindful of the privacy of your tenants. If you need to go to the property for inspection or maintenance, let them know ahead of time rather than make a surprise appearance.

**Honor the lease agreements:** This seems easy enough. You honor your end of the agreement and the tenants should honor their end. You cannot just evict someone from the property just because you don't like them.

**Keep the property safe:** Safety and security is important for your tenants and their neighbors. Make sure each property has working locks, so it prevents any burglaries or invasions of any kind. At the same time, check to see if the properties are not a place where crimes can be committed (like the production and sale of illegal drugs).

## Generating Extra Income and Reducing Expenses

This is the goal we all want, right? Extra income and less expenses. It's possible to get it done.

But the question is: how? Let's start with reducing expenses. There are plenty of ways to go about doing this.

Here are some examples on where you can reduce expenses:

## Fulfill vacancies quickly

The expenses add up when there are vacancies. Granted, once they are filled, those temporary expenses used to fulfill them will be off the books until the process needs to be repeated. Therefore, a fulfilled vacancy means more income and less of an expense.

## Do renovations when the time is right

If there are renovations that need to be done, do it whenever there are vacancies. This might be easy to do if you are renting out single family homes. From there, once the renovations are complete, this will give you a great window to increase the rent before the vacancy itself is fulfilled.

You must never increase the rent while there are tenants that are occupying the property. You don't want to put them in a financially precarious position where they feel like the need to make more just to make rent every month.

## Consider energy saving methods

You can save energy and a whole lot of money at the same time by doing some small tasks. These include cleaning the HVAC filters regularly, sealing any cracks around the windows and doors, keeping the temperature of the water heater down to a minimum, and installing LED light fixtures.

Also, you can install low flow shower heads and high-efficiency washers to save money on water. Efficiency is one of the best cost-effective ways to save money whether you are a property owner or a tenant.

### Consider alternative services

There may be a waste management service that provides less pickups for less money. This may be better than the other guy that does weekly pickups, but commands a high price. There may be a lawn care company that does mowing every month as opposed to every other week and charges you less for it.

Consider what might be the best alternative services to save a bit of money while keeping quality in mind. In other words, don't allow the property to let itself go just for the sake of saving extra money.

## Don't Forget to Manage Real Estate Taxes

If there is one thing you should never forget to do, it's the real estate taxes. If you forget to do them, not only will you fall behind financially, but you'll also find yourself missing out on a ton of awesome benefits and write-offs.

What are some real estate tax deductions you will possibly qualify for? Let's take a look at some of them:

**Cost for repairs, maintenance, and upkeep:** Yes, it pays to fix and maintain your properties. And that's why it's so important to keep a record of your expenses that are aimed towards it. The amount of sales taxes that you pay on all things repair and maintenance will definitely help you out in the long run once tax season comes. And you can even save a ton on your tax bill.

**Utilities:** Some utilities you have to pay for, and others will be the tenant's responsibility. Consider which utilities will be beneficial for your tax bill and go from there.

**Mortgage interest:** The interest that you pay on your mortgage will yield one of your best tax deductions yet. So, if you are paying off a mortgage, be sure to keep a record of how much interest you're paying on it. Also, if you have a mortgage insurance premium, you can get a tax deduction on that as well.

**Travel expenses:** You might have property on one end of town or in a different state. Either way, the travel costs such as gas and the like for going to and from your properties can count as a deduction on your taxes.

**Property tax deductions:** Don't forget, paying your property taxes on time will yield towards extra relief on your overall tax bill.

## Final Thoughts

Building your long-term wealth and your passive income via rental properties is possible. As long as you are taking the necessary steps, you'll be able to generate the amount of passive income and wealth you so desire. One thing to go about doing this is increasing your income while keeping expenses low.

Also, be sure to keep your business and personal expenses separate from one another so you avoid as much confusion as possible. Plus, keeping everything separate will make tax season a lot less frustrating. Remember, you can enlist the help of a CPA to help keep your finances in order.

Just because you have income rolling in the bank, doesn't mean you should just sit back and relax. You still have to take care of the business side of things such as checking on the properties and ensure that they are maintained. Not only that, but you also want to keep the tenants happy and listen to any issues they may have.

Remember, this is still a business that you need to tend to regularly. Sure, you can enjoy your financial freedom. But neglecting your business will lead to that financial freedom fading away.

# Chapter 15: If and When You Really Need to Exit, Here's What You Must Learn

Let's say you have amassed quite a bit of wealth over time. You've worked hard to put together a solid portfolio of rental properties. And now, it's time to move on and enjoy yourself.

In this chapter, we're going to be talking about exit strategies. When is a good time to exit? What should you do before executing your exit strategy?

There is more than one type of exit strategy that exists. And we'll be taking a look at each of them, so you'll know which one works best for you. There are also some mistakes that you need to avoid so the exit is smooth and seamless rather than filled with problems.

At this point, you have achieved your financial goals. Now, it's time to cash out and enjoy life after real estate. So, let's talk about exit strategies and everything you need to know about them:

## What Does It Mean to Exit?

To exit means to sell your rental properties if you want to move on with something else. In short, you are removing yourself from an investment deal. You could already be making money and decide that you've made enough to retire on.

Or maybe, you want to use a portion of the wealth you've amassed and use it to invest in something outside of real estate. With exit strategies, there's always an end goal. But still, it's important to plan it before executing it.

With this in mind, when should you consider an exit? You might not even be thinking about it during the time when you purchase the property. But at some point, once you already have a few properties under your belt, you might be thinking about the long-term future.

Yes, dealing with the rewards and risks of real estate for a long period of time can take a toll on people. And some landlords may feel burnt out by it all. Or, you may decide that it's time to wind down and start a new chapter in your life.

If you're young when you're starting out, you might be making plenty of money, and even retire at say age 40 or 45. From there, you can spend time with family or do some small ventures to help propel your retirement plan. If you are someone in your 30s or

40s, maybe you are looking to generate income from rental properties as a way to support your family for the long-term.

But when the time comes to exit, you'll think back and say that you've built something meaningful. You hate to let it go. But you are cashing in your chips and want to focus on what's next in your life, whatever that may be.

## Things to Consider Before Exiting

Before executing your exit strategy, you'll want to take a few things into consideration. Because you want the exit to be as smooth and issue-free as possible. What needs to be done before you finally are able to get the properties out of your hands?

Let's take a look at the following:

### Why now (or soon)?

The biggest question is why are you exiting now than perhaps later? This may be a personal question or perhaps you have other business plans and responsibilities that may require your full attention.

## Are my properties in good enough shape?

Before letting go of any property, you'll want to make sure that it is in good condition. Just like someone selling a house, they don't want to sell it to anyone who may be buying a piece of junk. So, you want to be considerate and sell it to someone who is getting a good property for what it's worth.

Just remember, if the property appears to be worn or in need of repair, you may be selling it for a lot less than what you paid for. And that will give you a loss rather than a gain.

## What does the current market look like?

How is the market looking at the moment? Are people looking to buy houses? How many people are selling their properties at the moment?

If the demand is healthy enough, you may move forward with your exit plan. However, you also want to check the supply as well. You may fare better in selling the property if there aren't a whole lot of properties up for sale at the same time.

If the market shows low demand and high supply, then you may want to hold off on your exit strategy until later on.

## Who will you sell the property to?

Will you sell the property to a homebuyer? Or will you sell it to another investor? At the end of the day, the buyer will do whatever they want with it.

This is entirely up to you. But if you see it still has the potential as a solid rental property, then by all means, sell it to a fellow investor. However, if you feel like a single-family home might just be a place that can be bought outright, then sell it to someone who wants to find a home.

## Is there any depreciation of the value?

Depreciation can kill an exit strategy dead. And it might take time before you recoup your losses by way of repairs or renovations. If the property value somehow depreciates, figure out what is causing it.

Also, find ways to increase the value so you can sell the property, even for a reduced price if it comes down to it.

## Do the maintenance costs cancel out the profits?

If the maintenance costs cancel out the profits, odds are it won't fare very well for anyone looking for a property that they're looking to rent out. At this point, it might be ideal to sell the property outright to a potential homeowner. If you are intending on selling it to an investor, be sure to find ways to cut down on maintenance costs so it's not a burden that is shouldered upon the new owner.

### Are there any issues affecting the cash flow?

As an outgoing owner, you want to be considerate of your fellow investors. If there is an issue regarding the cash flow of the property, figure out what it is and find an alternative solution. For example, you may be spending too much on a certain expense.

Therefore, it would be wise to make adjustments on said expenses to ensure a positive cash flow for the new owner.

## Learning Exit Strategies

We'll be taking a look at some of the common exit strategies that property investors can use. Since each differs from the other, we'll take a look at how each one works. From there, you can decide on which exit strategy will work for you best.

Let's take a look at the following:

## Fix and Flip

This is basically an exit strategy that is already implemented before you even buy a property. To explain this, you are purchasing a property (specifically a fixer-upper), repairing and rehabbing it, and then flipping it for a larger profit.

Since the property value has no place to go but up, you'll walk away with a nice tidy profit. You buy the property at below market value and sell at the purchase price plus repair costs. For example, if you buy the property at $100,000 and it costs you $75,000 to repair the property, then ideally you sell it at $175,000.

## Buy and Hold

This is usually one of the most used strategies. The way this works is you purchase the property and hold on to it for as long as possible. When the property value appreciates and you have built up enough equity, that's when you can sell it for a higher profit if you so choose.

## Selling it outright to a homeowner

If you have a single-family house or a townhome, then you have the option to sell it to a homeowner outright. This means the property will no longer be considered a rental property and will therefore become a private residence.

Before going down this route, be sure to make sure that the neighborhood that you're in has more homeowners than renters. If there are more renters than homeowners in the area, this kind of exit strategy will not work.

## Selling it to an investor

So, it comes full circle. One investor selling his property to another. You know exactly what will happen here and why the buyer is purchasing it.

Make sure the property is in an area where more people are renting as opposed to home-owning. The demand for homeowners and rental profits are different depending on the area that you're in.

## The 1031 Exchange

The 1031 Exchange is named after a part of the tax code (1031). The way the 1031 exchange works is where you swap one property with a 'like kind' property. If the exchange meets the 1031 requirements, there will be either no tax or limited tax that will be due around the time of the exchange.

In some situations, you may trade in a like-kind property and end up getting something in return that has far greater value. But don't count on that always being the case. Keep in mind that there is also a time slot in which the exchange must occur.

First, there is the 45-day rule. The sale of the property must occur within the first 45 days in order to qualify. You must designate the replacement property to the intermediary in writing with the correct address.

However, there is an additional rule known as the 180-day rule. If there is a deal, it must be closed within 180 days. This occurs in the event of a delayed exchange.

## Wholesaling

A wholesale deal is when a real estate investor acts as a middleman between the buyer and the seller. However, it's you that is the seller. So therefore, you are not the middleman in this setting.

The seller will have a purchase price like normal. However, the buyer must plan on purchasing it at a price higher than the listing price. The wholesaler will get the difference.

For example, if a seller's listing price is $250,000 and a buyer gets it for $275,000 then the wholesaler gets $25,000.

## Refinancing

Suppose you cannot sell to a homeowner nor an investor. What could possibly be the issue? The best solution would be to refinance the property.

Before you go down this road, make sure that your finances are in good shape. For example, make sure that your monthly rent is covering all expenses. Double check both your net operating income and your operating expenses.

After refinancing your property, try and sell the property again and see what happens.

## Avoid These Mistakes

Your exit strategy may hit a snag if you make some of these mistakes. Before you sell your properties and ride off into the sunset, here are some things you need to be aware of so you can prevent making these mistakes:

## Don't leave the place in bad shape

Simply put, you don't want to leave the property in worse shape than you found it. You worked hard enough for it to be a good rental property. Why let it go to waste?

Plus, you'll be screwing yourself out of a good deal if you allow the property to fall apart. Also, don't use it as an excuse to get out when you know full well that it is your responsibility to keep it clean and well-maintained.

## Leave the new investor with bad tenants

If you are selling the property with current tenants still occupying your property, be sure that the tenants are aware of the changes and what may follow. Be sure that they are still willing to pay the rent and follow the lease agreements.

The last thing the new investor wants is to deal with an inherited tenant that will end up being a headache.

## Take care of unexpected maintenance issues

Make sure that you perform one final inspection to see if there are any 'surprises' that need to be fixed.

Because a need for repairs and maintenance may pop out of nowhere. Be sure to nip it in the bud and take care of it before the property changes hands.

## Final Thoughts

Your exit strategy may take place years down the road. Or it may be a quick repair and flip. Either way, it's good to have one planned even before acquiring the property itself.

Consider your exit strategy options and choose which one will work for you best and why. And always avoid the mistakes listed above to ensure an orderly and proper transition of ownership between one investor or owner to the next.

# Conclusion

There you have it. You have just learned the ins and outs of building your rental property empire. At this point, you have either followed some of the steps already outlined or have yet to get started. Either way, no time is better than now to begin your journey towards making money with real estate.

You now have a basic understanding of the process of acquiring properties. You understand how there are various ways to receive financing. And you also have a process where you can repeat the process over and over again if you want to.

Remember, building a rental property empire is never easy. You know that it will take a few people to help get you there. These people are your mentors, your advisors, your partners, and your friends in the business.

It's important that you get your finances in order before making the first step if needed. If you haven't already, that should be the first thing you do. Soon after that, see what options are now available for financing.

After you've made a preliminary decision, you can then look for properties using the strategies and tactics outlined in Chapter 5. You also now have the know-how to make a good offer so you can land the property of your dreams. You don't have to be a master wheeler and dealer to get a good deal on a property.

Once the keys to the property are in your hands, you'll want to make some decisions on how to fix up the place before you rent it to a potential tenant. The more repairs and renovations you put together, the more value you'll add to the property.

Fixing up the property may require some DIY and professional contractor work. But you'll want to double check to see what fits in your repair and renovation plans before spending money on it. After the place looks nice and brand new, you can then rent it out to your ideal tenant.

This is a process that will get repeated over and over again as many times as you please. It can be with single-family homes, apartment complexes, townhomes, and more. It's a process that can be a challenge with every property you acquire or an easy one.

As always, be sure to build your real estate network from the ground up. Plus, you want to maintain it as best as you can. Communicate regularly with people in your network and connect those who are in need.

If someone is looking for a home loan, direct them to the loan officers you know. If a fellow real estate investor is looking for a contractor that remodels kitchens, give them a name. Your network will help you become the 'it person' to go to whenever something real estate related needs to be addressed.

Your tenants are the lifeblood of your rental property business. Without tenants, you will lose more money than you make. And if you don't get along with your tenants, they won't put in a good word for you if someone is asking for a place to rent.

Be sure to be on good terms with your tenants and be willing to handle any conflicts or repair requests whenever it's needed. With happy tenants, they'll be more than happy to help you out in looking for newer tenants when they move out.

At the same time, if you have vacancies to fulfill, get the word out. Because these vacancies can fill themselves. It's up to you to find the right tenant based on the application criteria.

When looking through applications, you want to make sure that they meet your requirements. Do background checks and make sure that they are the person that will give you an easy time rather than a hard one. Because tenants can cause trouble, damage the property, or have ridiculous demands.

It is possible to build long-term wealth with your rental properties. And you can earn plenty of passive income. However, treat your rental properties like a business rather than a hobby.

You still need to handle some of the other tasks such as maintaining the property, keeping the tenants happy, and making sure that everything is in good working condition. The properties are still your focus even if you are making plenty of money.

If you want to make as much money as possible, find ways to increase your income while keeping expenses low. There are plenty of ways to go about doing this. Find the best way without financially pinching your tenants.

And if you're ready to wrap it all up, be sure to have a good exit strategy in mind. You may fix and flip, buy and hold, or exchange it for a like-kind property via the 1031. Either way, choose an appropriate exit strategy that works for you.

After all this work you've put in and the actionable steps you've taken, you're well on your way to making money with rental properties. It doesn't get more satisfying knowing that you are on the path to absolute financial freedom.

What you do with the extra money you make is up to you. But don't let money change you in the slightest. Those who do will get complacent and may not care about their properties, thus allowing them to fall apart and lose tenants in the process.

## What's your greatest takeaway?

What are some great takeaways that you've learned from this book? Were there some things that you never knew about before reading this? What stuck out to you as most interesting?

We love to hear from you. Also, one more thing. We encourage you to keep this eBook as a reference guide.

Because if you are stuck on something, you can always refer to a specific chapter in the book. Don't let this be one of those books that you read once and be done with it. Oh, and we encourage you to share this book with someone who might be interested in rental properties as well.

# Resources

*4 Types of Real Estate and How to Profit from Each*. (2021). The Balance. https://www.thebalance.com/real-estate-what-it-is-and-how-it-works-3305882

*5 Popular Types of Rental Properties*. (2021). Best Rent. http://www.bestrent.vn/5-popular-types-of-rental-properties/

*15 Step Real Estate Due Diligence Checklist*. (2021, March 16). Financial Wolves. https://financialwolves.com/real-estate-due-diligence-checklist/

*1031 Exchange Rules: What You Need to Know*. (2021). Investopedia. https://www.investopedia.com/financial-edge/0110/10-things-to-know-about-1031-exchanges.aspx

A. (2019a, January 30). *How To Prepare My Property For Rent*. Madeleine Hicks Real Estate Brisbane. https://madeleinehicks.com.au/how-to-prepare-my-property-for-rent/

A. (2021a, February 12). *Loan to Cost vs. Loan to Value - Definitions*. HM Capital. https://hardmoola.com/loan-to-cost-vs-loan-to-value/

Agent Image. (2019, October 31). *Real Estate Marketing Strategies to Boost Your Online Presence and Turn Leads to Conversions*. Best Real Estate Websites for Agents and Brokers. https://www.agentimage.com/blog/5-real-estate-marketing-strategies-to-boost-your-online-presence-and-turn-leads-to-conversions/

Aiello, J. (2019, October 28). *How to Prepare Your Unit for a New Tenant*. Apartment Management Resources | Zumper. https://www.zumper.com/manage/resources/how-to-prepare-your-unit-for-a-new-tenant/

Aiello, J. (2020a, February 13). *What To Do If Your Rental Property Needs Repair*. Apartment Management Resources | Zumper. https://www.zumper.com/manage/resources/what-to-do-if-your-rental-property-needs-repair/

Aiello, J. (2020b, February 13). *What To Do If Your Rental Property Needs Repair*. Apartment Management Resources | Zumper.

https://www.zumper.com/manage/resources/what-to-do-if-your-rental-property-needs-repair/

B. (2020a, June 25). *20 Top Real Estate Investors Reveal Their Secrets for House Flipping and Wholesaling Success!* 7 Figure Flipping. https://7figureflipping.com/20-top-real-estate-investors-reveal-their-secrets-for-house-flipping-and-wholesaling-success/

Benson, A. (2020, October 26). *How to Make Money in Real Estate*. NerdWallet. https://www.nerdwallet.com/blog/investing/make-money-real-estate/

Brumer-Smith, L. (2020, February 10). *6 Ways to Earn More From Your Rental Property*. Millionacres. https://www.fool.com/millionacres/real-estate-investing/articles/6-ways-earn-more-your-rental-property/

Brumer-Smith, L. (2021, March 4). *Building a Cash Buyers List for Your Real Estate Investing Business*. Millionacres. https://www.fool.com/millionacres/real-estate-investing/building-a-cash-buyers-list-for-your-real-estate-investing-business/

Bryant, C. W. (2020, January 27). *How Foreclosures Work*. HowStuffWorks. https://money.howstuffworks.com/personal-finance/debt-management/foreclosure.htm

C. (2019b, August 8). *Top 5 Tips for Effective Communication in Real Estate - MyBayut*. A Blog about Homes, Trends, Tips & Life in the UAE | MyBayut. https://www.bayut.com/mybayut/tips-effective-communication-real-estate-clients/

Carson, C. (2016, December 21). *6 Reasons I Prefer Creative Financing to Bank Financing*. Coach Carson. https://www.coachcarson.com/6-reasons-i-prefer-creative-financing-to-bank-financing/

Chandler, D. (2018, October 3). *Multifamily homes: Make your house pay for itself*. Mortgage Rates, Mortgage News and Strategy : The Mortgage Reports. https://themortgagereports.com/27635/multifamily-homes-make-your-house-pay-for-itself

Chang, J. (2021, March 16). *How Much to Charge for Rent in 2020: A Landlord's Guide | BiggerPockets*. The BiggerPockets Blog | Real Estate Investing & Personal Finance Advice.

https://www.biggerpockets.com/blog/how-much-to-charge-for-rent

Corporate Finance Institute. (2020, April 23). *Real Estate*. https://corporatefinanceinstitute.com/resources/careers/jobs/real-estate/

*DIY Plumbing vs Hiring a Professional - BFP Bay Area*. (2017, June 28). Benjamin Franklin Plumbing, Inc. https://bfplumbingbayarea.com/blog/diy-plumbing-vs-hiring-a-professional/

*Do you have an accountability partner on your side?* (2016, July 15). Inman. https://www.inman.com/2016/07/15/do-you-have-an-accountability-partner-on-your-side/

Esajian, J. D. (2021, February 26). *BRRRR Strategy*. FortuneBuilders. https://www.fortunebuilders.com/brrrr-strategy/

*First-Time Home Buyer Checklist | Property Inspection & More*. (2021). Mr. Handyman. https://www.mrhandyman.com/tips-ideas/checklists-resources/first-time-home-buyer-checklist/

Foy, N. (2020, April 16). *The Ultimate Guide to Financing Real Estate Investment Purchases*. Under 30 Wealth. https://under30wealth.com/the-ultimate-guide-to-financing-real-estate-investments/

Frankel, M. C. (2021, February 4). *How to Make Money in Real Estate*. Millionacres. https://www.fool.com/millionacres/real-estate-basics/investing-basics/how-to-make-money-in-real-estate/

G. (2019c, September 3). *How to Evaluate a Real Estate Investment*. Above the Canopy. https://www.abovethecanopy.us/how-to-evaluate-a-real-estate-investment/

G. (2019d, September 3). *How to Evaluate a Real Estate Investment*. Above the Canopy. https://www.abovethecanopy.us/how-to-evaluate-a-real-estate-investment/

Gerardo, P. (2019, September 17). *You want to fire your real estate agent. Can you do that?* Mortgage Rates, Mortgage News and Strategy : The Mortgage Reports. https://themortgagereports.com/37074/fire-your-real-estate-agent

Gerardo, P. (2021, March 2). *Avoid these 7 mistakes when making an offer on a house*. Mortgage Rates, Mortgage News and Strategy : The Mortgage Reports. https://themortgagereports.com/38667/avoid-these-7-mistakes-when-making-an-offer-on-a-house

Hall, B. (2021, March 16). *Is Renting to Family a Good Idea? Beware of the "Personal Use" Trap*. The BiggerPockets Blog | Real Estate Investing & Personal Finance Advice. https://www.biggerpockets.com/blog/renting-to-family

Hamed, E. (2018, March 11). *Buying a Rental Property Below Market Value*. Investment Property Tips | Mashvisor Real Estate Blog. https://www.mashvisor.com/blog/buying-a-rental-property-below-market-value/

*How can I look for rental housing?* (2021). Settlement. https://settlement.org/ontario/housing/rent-a-home/find-rental-housing/how-can-i-look-for-rental-housing/

*How Much Money Do You Need To Invest In Real Estate?* (2021). Investopedia. https://www.investopedia.com/financial-edge/0712/how-much-money-do-you-need-to-invest-in-real-estate.aspx

*How the Fair Housing Act Prevents Discrimination*. (2021). The Balance Small Business. https://www.thebalancesmb.com/what-is-the-federal-fair-housing-act-2125014

*How To Advertise Your Rental Property: Step-By-Step Guide*. (2020, October 19). RentPrep. https://rentprep.com/tenant-screening/advertise-rental-property/

*How to Build And Maintain Cash Reserves For Your Rental Property*. (2021). Real Life Planning. https://reallifeplanning.com/blog/how-to-build-and-maintain-cash-reserves-for-your-rental-property

*How to create the right team of commercial real estate advisors*. (2020, September 12). BDC.Ca. https://www.bdc.ca/en/articles-tools/money-finance/buy-lease-commercial-real-estate/how-get-right-team-commercial-real-estate-advisors

*How to Hire a Handyman for Rental Property*. (2018a, December 21). Rental Resources |

RentPost.
https://rentpost.com/resources/article/hire-a-handyman-for-rental-property/

*How to Hire a Handyman for Rental Property*. (2018b, December 21). Rental Resources | RentPost.
https://rentpost.com/resources/article/hire-a-handyman-for-rental-property/

*How To Use Rental Income To Build Long-Term Wealth*. (2018, September 15). VerraTerra. https://www.verraterra.com/how-to-use-rental-income-to-build-long-term-wealth/

Huber, J. (2021, February 9). *Should I Repair or Replace My Roof?* Huber & Associates.
https://www.huberroofing.com/blog/2018/4/13/should-i-repair-or-replace-my-roof

Income, P. (2020, May 12). *Use Leverage to Purchase Properties*. Passive Income M.D.
https://passiveincomemd.com/use-leverage-to-purchase-properties/

*Investing in Rental Properties for Beginners*. (2021). Realty Mogul.
https://www.realtymogul.com/knowledge-center/article/investing-rental-properties-beginners

Jan, O. A. (2019, June 10). *Real Estate Valuation*. XPLAIND.Com. https://xplaind.com/726953/real-estate-valuation

K. (2020b, June 25). *How Rental Property Financing Gives You Investment Leverage*. HomeUnion. https://www.homeunion.com/how-financing-a-rental-property-gives-you-leverage-in-real-estate-investments/

K. (2020c, June 25). *How Rental Property Financing Gives You Investment Leverage*. HomeUnion. https://www.homeunion.com/how-financing-a-rental-property-gives-you-leverage-in-real-estate-investments/

*Landlord and renters insurance*. (2021). Understand Insurance. https://understandinsurance.com.au/types-of-insurance/landlord-and-renters-insurance

*Landlord Characteristics and Responsibilities*. (2021). The Balance Small Business. https://www.thebalancesmb.com/what-is-a-landlord-duties-and-responsibilities-2125057

Lee, M. (2020, November 11). *DIY Flooring: Should I Install My Flooring Myself or Hire a Professional? | BuildDirect® Blog*. BuildDirect

Blog: Life at Home. https://www.builddirect.com/blog/diy-flooring-should-i-install-my-flooring-myself-or-hire-a-professional/

Leusin, Y. (2019, March 2). *Owning Rental Properties: 4 Challenges and Their Solutions*. Investment Property Tips | Mashvisor Real Estate Blog. https://www.mashvisor.com/blog/owning-rental-properties-challenges-solutions/

Lofgren, L. (2021, March 1). *The Best Property Management Software – 2021 Review*. QuickSprout. https://www.quicksprout.com/best-property-management-software/

Lucas, T. (2018, November 30). *What happens when my real estate offer is accepted? [Video]*. Mortgage Rates, Mortgage News and Strategy : The Mortgage Reports. https://themortgagereports.com/45667/what-happens-when-my-real-estate-offer-is-accepted

Luxon, B. (2020a, November 4). *Key Figures For Evaluating An Investment Property*. Landlord Studio.

https://www.landlordstudio.com/blog/key-figures-for-evaluating-an-investment-property/

Luxon, B. (2020b, November 4). *The Landlords Guide To Successful House Hacking*. Landlord Studio. https://www.landlordstudio.com/blog/the-landlords-guide-to-successful-house-hacking/

Marrs, M. (2020, June 24). *35 Easy & Effective Real Estate Marketing Ideas*. WordStream. https://www.wordstream.com/blog/ws/2015/04/16/real-estate-marketing

Martin, E. J. (2018, October 19). *How do I finalize my offer to buy a home?* Mortgage Rates, Mortgage News and Strategy : The Mortgage Reports. https://themortgagereports.com/39613/how-do-i-finalize-my-offer-to-buy-a-home

Martin, E. J. (2019, September 17). *What is "recording" when closing on a home purchase?* Mortgage Rates, Mortgage News and Strategy : The Mortgage Reports. https://themortgagereports.com/37838/closing-real-estate-recording-fees

Martin, E. J. (2020, September 3). *Understanding a real estate contract or purchase agreement*. Mortgage Rates, Mortgage News and Strategy : The Mortgage Reports. https://themortgagereports.com/37569/understanding-a-real-estate-contract-or-purchase-agreement

Maughan, J. (2018, January 17). *How to Handle Inherited Tenants*. RentPrep. https://rentprep.com/facebook/how-to-handle-inherited-tenants/

Merrill, T. (2020, November 13). *A Beginner's Guide To Starting A Real Estate Business*. FortuneBuilders. https://www.fortunebuilders.com/a-beginners-guide-to-starting-a-real-estate-business/

Miller, M. (2018, June 13). *Is It Time to Hire Employees for Your Real Estate Investment Business?* 5 Arch. https://5archfunding.com/blog/is-it-time-to-hire-employees-for-your-real-estate-investment-business/

Miller, P. (2019, September 17). *Home closing: What you need to read, what you can skim*. Mortgage Rates, Mortgage News and Strategy : The Mortgage Reports. https://themortgagereports.com/39671/home-closing-what-you-need-to-read-what-you-can-skim

Mizes, B. (2020, April 24). *How to Overcome the 5 Challenges of Owning Rental Property*. National Landlord Association (NLA). https://www.nationallandlordassociation.org/how-to-overcome-the-5-challenges-of-owning-rental-property/

Moran, G. (2015, November 19). *8 costs to consider when buying a rental property*. Hsh.Com. https://www.hsh.com/finance/real-estate/costs-to-consider-when-buying-rental-property.html

N. (2021b, March 19). *Bank loans*. Nav. https://www.nav.com/business-financing-options/bank-loans/

Patel, K. (2018, February 5). *5 Key Numbers to Know for Any Kind of Real Estate Investment*. Copyright (c)2004-2021 BiggerPockets, LLC. https://www.biggerpockets.com/member-blogs/10401/70423-5-key-numbers-to-know-for-any-kind-of-real-estate-investment

R., A. (2020, August 20). *Top 5 Tenant Communication Tips for Landlords*.

DialMyCalls. https://www.dialmycalls.com/blog/top-5-tenant-communication-tips-landlords

Ragan, B. (2021, February 23). *Should I Repair My Roof or Replace It?* Bill Ragan Roofing. https://www.billraganroofing.com/blog/should-i-repair-my-roof-or-replace-it

*Real Estate Definition*. (2021). Investopedia. https://www.investopedia.com/terms/r/realestate.asp

*Real Estate Taxes 101: Rental Property Tax Deductions*. (2020, September 9). HomeUnion. https://www.homeunion.com/how-to-claim-real-estate-taxes-and-deductions/

*Rental Property Renovations to Attract Tenants*. (2021). Dumpsters. https://www.dumpsters.com/blog/renovating-a-rental-property

*Rentometer: How to Increase Storage Options in Small Rental Properties*. (2021). Rentometer. https://www.rentometer.com/articles/how-to-increase-storage-options-in-small-rental-properties

*Richey Property Management, LLC*. (2021). Richey Property Management. https://www.richeypm.com/rental-application-process

Roeling, T. (2021, March 16). *Tenant Abandonment Guide for Landlords*. TurboTenant. https://www.turbotenant.com/blog/tenant-abandonment-guide/

Roos, L. A. O. D. (2021, February 10). *How Buying a House Works*. HowStuffWorks. https://home.howstuffworks.com/real-estate/buying-home/house-buying.htm

Santarelli, M. (2021, March 11). *How To Make Money In Real Estate And Get Rich In 2021?* Norada Real Estate Investments. https://www.noradarealestate.com/blog/how-to-make-money-in-real-estate/

Scott, J. (2021, March 29). *Real Estate Investment Analysis: Step-by-Step Guide*. The BiggerPockets Blog | Real Estate Investing & Personal Finance Advice. https://www.biggerpockets.com/blog/real-estate-investment-analysis

*Screening to Get the Best Tenants for Your Rental Property | Mynd Management*. (2021). MYND Management. https://www.mynd.co/knowledge-center/screening-to-get-the-best-tenants

*Should You Be Investing in Real Estate?* (2021). The Balance. https://www.thebalance.com/real-estate-investing-101-357985

Siddons, S. (2021, February 12). *How Real Estate Investment Clubs Work*. HowStuffWorks. https://home.howstuffworks.com/real-estate/buying-home/real-estate-investment-clubs.htm

*Six Types of Problem Tenants – and How to Deal With Them*. (2020, June 9). Propertyware. https://www.propertyware.com/blog/six-types-of-problem-tenants-and-how-to-deal-with-them/

Solutions, R. (2020, April 22). *How to Make an Offer on a House*. Daveramsey.Com. https://www.daveramsey.com/blog/how-to-make-an-offer

Solutions, R. (2021, February 24). *How to Find a Real Estate Agent*. Daveramsey.Com. https://www.daveramsey.com/blog/how-to-find-a-real-estate-agent

Syrios, A. (2021, March 16). *13 Ways To Increase Rent & Value To Your Rental Property | Blog*. The BiggerPockets Blog | Real Estate Investing & Personal Finance Advice. https://www.biggerpockets.com/blog/13-ways-increase-rent-add-rental-property

T. (2013, September 26). *10 Ways for Landlords to Avoid Tenant Legal Claims*. Anco. https://www.anco.com/blog/10-ways-landlords-avoid-tenant-legal-claims/

T. (2021c, January 28). *Landlord Tax Tips: Hiring Family Members is a Win-Win*. AAOA. https://www.american-apartment-owners-association.org/property-management/latest-news/landlord-tax-tips-hiring-family-members-is-a-win-win/

*Tenant Vacating Checklist for Landlords*. (2021). The Balance Small Business. https://www.thebalancesmb.com/sample-move-out-checklist-for-landlords-and-tenants-2125000

*The 5 Best Real Estate Marketing Tools to Use in 2019*. (2021). EZ Texting. https://www.eztexting.com/blog/5-best-real-estate-marketing-tools-use-2019

*The Big List of Real Estate Scams, Fraud, and Misleading Tactics*. (2021). Kris Lindahl. https://www.krislindahl.com/real-estate-scams-fraud-and-misleading-tactics.php

*The dos and don'ts of landscaping on rental properties*. (2021, March 8). Total Landscape Care. https://www.totallandscapecare.com/business/article/15042222/the-dos-and-donts-of-landscaping-on-rental-properties

*The Homeowner's Guide to Interior Demolition*. (2021). Hometown Demolition. https://www.hometowndemolitioncontractors.com/blog/homeowners-guide-to-interior-demolition

*Time Management Tips for Busy Property Managers*. (2021). Renters Warehouse. https://renterswarehouse.com/education/time-management-tips-busy-property-managers

Treger, T. (2020, February 24). *Real Estate Due Diligence: A Simple Guide for Investment*

*Properties*. Financial Poise. https://www.financialpoise.com/real-estate-due-diligence/

Turner, B. (2021, March 16). *The 11 Most Common Questions Asked by Tenants—Answered.* The BiggerPockets Blog | Real Estate Investing & Personal Finance Advice. https://www.biggerpockets.com/blog/11-common-questions-asked-tenants-answered

*Undecided About DIYing or Hiring a Pro? This Chart Tells All*. (2021). The Spruce. https://www.thespruce.com/remodel-myself-or-hire-pro-1822421

Warden, P. (2019a, March 8). *Open houses: What's their role in the home-buying process?* Mortgage Rates, Mortgage News and Strategy : The Mortgage Reports. https://themortgagereports.com/37900/open-houses-whats-their-role-in-the-home-buying-process

Warden, P. (2019b, September 17). *How to get out of a real estate contract*. Mortgage Rates, Mortgage News and Strategy : The Mortgage Reports. https://themortgagereports.com/37472/can-you-back-out-of-an-offer-to-buy-a-home

Weber, J. L. (2020, February 10). *How to Make a Construction Schedule*. ProjectManager.Com. https://www.projectmanager.com/blog/make-a-construction-schedule

Welles, H. (2019, August 22). *5 Ways to Communicate Better with Challenging Tenants*. Rental Housing Journal. https://rentalhousingjournal.com/5-ways-to-communicate-better-with-challenging-tenants/

*What to Consider When Self-Managing Your Rental Property*. (2021). Wilmington For Rent. https://www.wilmingtonforrent.com/blog/what-to-consider-when-self-managing-your-rental-property

White, S. M. (2018, June 12). *What to Do If a Tenant Dies in Your Rental Property*. RentPrep. https://rentprep.com/property-management/tenant-dies-your-rental-property/

*Why Reserve Funds Are Important When Managing A Property*. (2021). Lofty Real Estate. https://www.loftyrealestate.com/property-management/why-reserve-funds-are-important-when-managing-a-property/

Wilson, C. (2019, April 1). *Real Estate Negotiation Tips for Home Buyers and Sellers*. Homesnap. https://blog.homesnap.com/real-estate-negotiation-tips-for-home-buyers-and-sellers/

www.ingramcontent.com/pod-product-compliance
Lightning Source LLC
LaVergne TN
LVHW010319220926
848484LV00004BB/795